EVALUATING TRAINING

Latest titles in the McGraw-Hill Training Series

EVALUATING TRAINING EFFECTIVENESS 2nd edition
Benchmarking your Training Activity Against Best Practice
Peter Bramley   ISBN 0-07-709028-4
DEVELOPING A LEARNING CULTURE
Empowering People to Deliver Quality, Innovation and Long-term Success
Sue Jones   ISBN 0-07-707983-3
THE CREATIVE TRAINER
Holistic Facilitation Skills for Accelerated Learning
Michael Lawlor and Peter Handley   ISBN 0-07-709030-6
DEVELOPING EFFECTIVE TRAINING SKILLS 2nd edition
A Practical Guide to Designing and Delivering Group Training
Tony Pont   ISBN 0-07-709143-4
CROSS-CULTURAL TEAM BUILDING
Guidelines for More Effective Communication and Negotiation
Mel Berger   ISBN 0-07-707919-1
LEARNING TO CHANGE
A Resource for Trainers, Managers and Learners Based on Self-Organized Learning
Sheila Harri-Augstein and Ian M. Webb   ISBN 0-07-707896-9
ASSESSMENT AND DEVELOPMENT IN EUROPE
Adding Value to Individuals and Organizations
Edited by Mac Bolton   ISBN 0-07-707928-0
PRACTICAL INSTRUCTIONAL DESIGN FOR OPEN LEARNING
MATERIALS
A Modular Course Covering Open Learning, Computer-based Training and Multi-
media
Nigel Harrison   ISBN 0-07-709055-1
DELIVERING IN-HOUSE OUTPLACEMENT
A Practical Guide for Trainers, Managers and Personnel Specialists
Alan Jones   ISBN 0-07-707895-0
FACILITATION
Providing Opportunities For Learning
Trevor Bentley   ISBN 0-07-707684-2
DEVELOPMENT CENTRES
Realizing the Potential of Your Employees Through Assessment and Development
Geoff Lee and David Beard   ISBN 0-07-707785-7
DEVELOPING DIRECTORS
Building an Effective Boardroom Team
Colin Coulson-Thomas   ISBN 0-07-707590-0
MANAGING THE TRAINING PROCESS
Putting the Basics into Practice
Mike Wills   ISBN 0-07-707806-3
RESOURCE-BASED LEARNING
Using Open and Flexible Resources for Continuous Development
Julie Dorrell   ISBN 0-07-707692-3

Details of these and other titles in the series are available from:

The Product Manager, Professional Books, McGraw-Hill Publishing Company,
Shoppenhangers Road, Maidenhead, Berkshire SL6 2QL, United Kingdom
Tel: 01628 23432 Fax: 01628 770224

Evaluating training effectiveness

SECOND EDITION

Benchmarking your training activity against best practice

Peter Bramley

The McGraw-Hill Companies

London · New York · St Louis · San Francisco · Auckland
Bogotá · Caracas · Lisbon · Madrid · Mexico · Milan
Montreal · New Delhi · Panama · Paris · San Juan · São Paulo
Singapore · Sydney · Tokyo · Toronto

Published by
McGRAW-HILL Publishing Company
Shoppenhangers Road, Maidenhead, Berkshire, SL6 2QL, England
Telephone: 01628 23432
Fax: 01628 770224

British Library Cataloguing in Publication Data
Bramley, Peter
 Evaluating Training Effectiveness:
 Benchmarking Your Training Activity
 Against Best Practice.–2Rev.ed.–
 (Training Series)
 I. Title   II. Series
 658.312404

Reprinted 1997

ISBN 0-07-709028-4

Library of Congress Cataloging-in-Publication Data
Bramley, Peter,
 Evaluating training effectiveness: benchmarking your training
activity against best practice / Peter Bramley.–2nd ed.
  p.   cm.
 Includes bibliographical references and index.
 ISBN 0-07-709028-4 (pbk. : alk. paper)
 1. Employees–Training of–Evaluation.   I. Title.
HF5549.5.T7B63   1996
658.3'12404–dc20   95-43784
                                                                CIP

McGraw-Hill

A Division of The **McGraw·Hill** Companies

Typeset by BookEns Limited, Royston, Herts.
and printed and bound in Great Britain at the University Press, Cambridge.

Printed on permanent paper in compliance with ISO Standard 9706

Contents

Series preface

Training and development are now firmly centre stage in most organizations, if not all. Nothing unusual in that—for some organizations. They have always seen training and development as part of the heart of their businesses—but more and more must see it that same way.

The demographic trends through the 1990s will inject into the marketplace severe competition for good people who will need good training. Young people without conventional qualifications, skilled workers in redundant crafts, people out of work, women wishing to return to work—all will require excellent training to fit them to meet the job demands of the 1990s and beyond.

But excellent training does not spring from what we have done well in the past. T&D specialists are in a new ball game. 'Maintenance' training—training to keep up skill levels to do what we have always done—will be less in demand. Rather, organization, work and market change training are now much more important and will remain so for some time. Changing organizations and people is no easy task, requiring special skills and expertise which, sadly, many T&D specialists do not possess.

To work as a 'change' specialist requires us to get to centre stage—to the heart of the company's business. This means we have to ask about future goals and strategies, and even be involved in their development, at least as far as T&D policies are concerned.

This demands excellent communication skills, political expertise, negotiating ability, diagnostic skills—indeed, all the skills a good internal consultant requires.

The implications for T&D specialists are considerable. It is not enough merely to be skilled in the basics of training, we must also begin to act like business people and to think in business terms and talk the language of business. We must be able to resource training not just from within but by using the vast array of external resources. We must be able to manage our activities as well as any other manager. We must share in the creation and communication of the company's vision. We must never let the goals of the company out of our sight.

In short, we may have to grow and change with the business. It will be hard. We shall have to demonstrate not only relevance but also value for money and achievement of results. We shall be our own boss, as accountable for results as any other line manager, and we shall have to deal with fewer internal resources.

The challenge is on, as many T&D specialists have demonstrated to me over the past few years. We need to be capable of meeting that challenge. This is why McGraw-Hill Book Company Europe have planned and launched this major new training series—to help us meet that challenge.

The series covers all aspects of T&D and provides the knowledge base from which we can develop plans to meet the challenge. They are practical books for the professional person. They are a starting point for planning our journey into the twenty-first century.

Use them well. Don't just read them. Highlight key ideas, thoughts, action pointers or whatever, and have a go at doing something with them. Through experimentation we evolve; through stagnation we die.

I know that all the authors in the McGraw-Hill Training Series would want me to wish you good luck. Have a great journey into the twenty-first century.

ROGER BENNETT
Series Editor

About the series editor

Roger Bennett has over 20 years' experience in training, management education, research and consulting. He has long been involved with trainer training and trainer effectiveness. He has carried out research into trainer effectiveness, and conducted workshops, seminars, and conferences on the subject around the world. He has written extensively on the subject including the book *Improving Trainer Effectiveness*, Gower. His work has taken him all over the world and has involved directors of companies as well as managers and trainers.

Dr Bennett has worked in engineering, several business schools (including the International Management Centre, where he launched the UK's first masters degree in T&D), and has been a board director of two companies. He is the editor of the *Journal of European Industrial Training* and was series editor of the ITD's *Get In There* workbook and video package for the managers of training departments. He now runs his own business called The Management Development Consultancy.

Acknowledgements

I would like to express my thanks to Brenda Moran and Ruth Nissim for their help and encouragement during the preparation of this book. They both read the draft and suggested many ways in which the ideas could be better expressed. Their comments have forced me to think more clearly and the final product has been enriched by their contributions.

Introduction

Since the first edition was published, interest in evaluation, particularly in the UK, has intensified. The government has set the tone by requiring the evaluation of virtually everything in the public sector through a variety of forms of enhanced accountability, including competitive tendering. Organizations in both the public and private sectors have faced increasing demands for standards and quality and the ability to demonstrate, both to customers and regulators, the achievement of both.

Similarly, within organizations, training managers have been confronted with sharpened expectations. No longer can a training budget, no matter how small, be taken for granted. Now, to win or retain their budget, training professionals must carve out a positive role in organizational plans, winning resources by demonstrating the links between training plans and corporate objectives and establish the value of these plans once implemented. Staff development is one priority among many and must compete with others to show a sound return on investment.

In some organizations, a commitment to a 'Total Quality Management' process provides a framework within which training and development are planned, delivered and quality assured. In a growing number, the 'Investors in People' award has been set as the goal. Its success is based upon the simplicity of its formula—commitment, planning, action and evaluation. Simple or not, it is a challenge for many small and medium-sized (and even some large) organizations to meet, and many training managers have been faced, for the first time, with the sizeable task of showing how development activity has been evaluated. A further development has been the increased interest in the National Training Awards, which have provided an opportunity each year for organizations which have been able to demonstrate a business return on training investment to gain public recognition.

Traditional areas of training have also changed since the first edition was published. Most of the UK management schools have seen a steep decline in the nominations for public courses and have adapted by increasing the number of tailor-made in-company programmes which offer alternative benefits. The survey 'Training in Britain' showed that about half of the training delivered in the UK during 1986/87 was 'on-the-job'. The section on evaluating changes in effectiveness has been expanded to reflect these changes.

My own focus on evaluation has also altered as I have become more aware of its function as a political process and less convinced of its claims to be 'science'. Most of the section on the purpose of, and strategies for, evaluation reflects this shift towards the need to reconcile the conflicting aims and interests of different stakeholders. The sections on responsive evaluation and presenting an evaluation report have been expanded too.

Theoretical advances have also been made during the past four years. There has been a comprehensive review of the literature on training and development by Tannenbaum and Yukl (1992), and a new edition of the *Handbook of Industrial and Organizational Psychology* (Dunnette and Hough, 1992). There have also been a number of articles and research papers on evaluation, transfer of learning and self-efficacy. It is therefore time to revise a book which attempts to translate theory into practicality.

Training efficiency and effectiveness

When organizations ask for my help in evaluating their training activities they usually want to know whether the training was efficient, i.e. whether the programme achieved most of its objectives in a reasonably economic way. This question can be quite simply answered by assessing the changes achieved during training and perhaps by examining the process.

If an organization were to pose the more difficult question, 'Was the training effective?', this would involve a more complex analysis. It would imply not only finding out whether the training was well done but also asking what it achieved and whether it was worth while for the organization to be sponsoring it.

Definitions of training

Now one might expect the value of training to be assessed like that of other organizational functions; that is, by its contribution to organizational goals. The fact that organizations are asking the first type of question (about efficiency) rather than the second type (about effectiveness) is a consequence of their definition of training which assumes that it is a process of adding to the skills of an individual. Using such a definition makes it difficult for them to formulate questions about changes in organizational effectiveness or contributions to organizational goals when thinking about the evaluation of training.

The process of training employees within an organizational context is defined in different ways by different authors. Two typical definitions are given here to emphasize that clarity of definition is necessary because this controls the questions which can legitimately be raised.

A typical British definition is offered by the Department of Employment *Glossary of Training Terms* (1981): 'The systematic development of the attitude/knowledge/skill/behaviour pattern required by an individual to perform adequately a given task or job'.

The key concepts here are:

- 'Systematic development', which implies planning and control
- 'Individual', which excludes group and team development
- Job or task performance, which is the criterion of success.

One can see a strong link between this definition and the long tradition of industrial, technical training which is part of our culture. The definition has strengths in that it emphasizes a systematic process for improving work-based performance. Its weakness, for me, is that by excluding groups and teams it ignores important aspects of the organizational context.

A typical American definition is very different, for instance the one offered by Hinrichs (1976) is: 'Any organizationally initiated procedures which are intended to foster learning among organizational members in a direction contributing to organizational effectiveness'.

The key concepts are:

- 'Organizational procedures', which put the process into an organizational context
- 'Foster learning', which implies that the responsibility is shared between the organization offering it and the members receiving it
- The criterion of success is 'organizational effectiveness'.

This definition is much broader than the previous one and it would allow the inclusion of many organizational development activities as well as technical training. The strength of the definition is that it firmly plants training in its organizational context.

The synthesis of the necessary core concepts which I draw from these definitions and others like them can be summarized in the following statements:

1 Training should be a systematic process with some planning and control rather than random learning from experience.
2 It should be concerned with changing concepts, skills or attitudes of people treated both as individuals and as groups.
3 It is intended to improve performance in both the present and the following job and through this should enhance the effectiveness of the part of the organization where the individual or group works.

Implications for evaluation

These concepts underpin the logic which has provided the structure for this book. The examination of the process and changes achieved is necessary when evaluating training, and this will answer questions about *efficiency*. The key question which is addressed in Part Two of this book is, 'How will our training processes be judged if they are benchmarked against examples of best practice?' Part Three of the book addresses the question, 'How can we measure changes in knowledge, skills, attitudes and behaviour which might result from learning activities?'

Statement 3 above implies that training in organizations must include assessments of improvements in individual and organizational performance. This means asking questions about *effectiveness*. The last two sections of Part Three of the book address this issue and provide help with which to answer the following questions:

'Is the training which is being provided of direct benefit in increasing the ability to do the work and meet objectives?'
'Is training improving aspects of organizational effectiveness? How could we demonstrate that?'
'How might we strengthen the link between the objectives for training and the current organizational priorities or business plans?'
'How might we involve line managers in the training process to ensure more effective training and a better link between off-job and on-job development activities?'

The title of the book is *Evaluating Training Effectiveness* and this is a deliberate choice of words. It is not possible to divorce training in organizations from the concept of effectiveness. Nor can the concept of evaluation be separated from the training process.

In tracing the development of my ideas, looking at both theoretical and practical contributions, I am hoping to offer readers a framework in which to conceptualize their own knowledge and experience. This should make it possible for the reader to go back into the organizational context and ask different questions. Asking different questions is the first step in promoting the process of change.

PART ONE

Why evaluate training?

Introduction

In the Introduction many of the reasons why evaluation should be carried out have been discussed. Now we turn to the various purposes which it can serve and the different approaches through which these purposes can be met. Before we become too deeply involved in this, it would be worth while for you to consider what your views are with respect to evaluation. What sort of process do you think that it should be? Figure 1 offers a set of seven-point scales with anchors at each end. We suggest that you select a point on each scale line which represents your opinion with regard to the process of evaluation.

Evaluation of training *should* be:

Helping the management to inspect training	1 2 3 4 5 6 7	Helping the trainers to develop activities
An assessment process which leads to recommendations	1 2 3 4 5 6 7	Non-judgemental and therefore likely to pose questions
Statistical and scientific, as its primary concern is with objective measurement	1 2 3 4 5 6 7	Anecdotal and descriptive, as its primary concern is with subjective interpretation
A carefully planned process with a set agenda	1 2 3 4 5 6 7	Changing throughout as the focus changes during the process
Estimating the worth of training activities to the organization	1 2 3 4 5 6 7	Providing feedback to the training department

| Based on large Based on small samples and asking quite simple questions in-depth questioning | 1 2 3 4 5 6 7 | samples and using |
| Part of the process for all training activities about a programme | 1 2 3 4 5 6 7 | Carried out only when there is some doubt |

Figure 1　*Views on the process of evaluation*
(Adapted from an idea by Len Gill, Merseyside Police)

The left-hand side of these scales represents a view that the main purpose of evaluation is to assess the worth of training to the organization and that this is best done by quantitative methods incorporated into a scientific approach. The right-hand side is quite close to research on methods of learning, where the quality of the experience, as reported by those involved, is the main focus. Many trainers can see the value of both these positions and hope that evaluation will satisfy both purposes. As we shall see, this is difficult to achieve. Particular forms of evaluation can be designed to meet particular purposes, but it is necessary to be clear about what the purpose is before embarking on the process.

1 Purposes of evaluation

The most common view of evaluation is that it completes the cycle of training. My view is that it is integral to the cycle and has the key role of quality control of the cycle by providing feedback on:

- the effectiveness of the methods being used
- the achievement of the objectives set by both trainers and trainees
- whether the needs originally identified, both at organizational and individual level, have been met.

It should be clear, from inspection of the cycle in Figure 1.1, that the criteria against which to evaluate need to be established before the design of the learning situations.

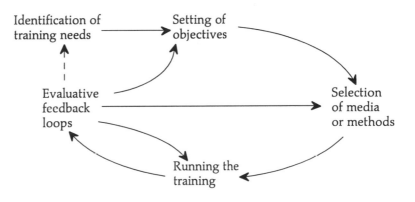

Figure 1.1 *The training cycle*

Goldstein (1993, page 147) defines evaluation as: 'The systematic collection of descriptive and judgemental information necessary to make effective decisions related to the selection, adoption, value and modification of various instructional activities'. I consider this definition to be particularly valuable as it implies that evaluation is a set of information-gathering techniques. Furthermore, that the selection of a particular strategy or technique, or of the particular aspect of the learning process which is examined, will vary with the purpose for which the evaluation is intended. Various purposes have been proposed by different authors.

Easterby-Smith (1986, page 13) offers three general purposes for evaluation: proving, improving and learning.

Proving aims 'to demonstrate conclusively that something has happened as a result of training or developmental activities'.

Improving implies 'an emphasis on trying to ensure that either the current or future programmes and activities become better than they are at present'.

Learning recognizes that 'evaluation cannot be divorced from the processes on which it concentrates ... and is an integral part of the learning and development process itself'.

(In the 1994 second edition, he also includes *control*.)

I prefer a rather different grouping of five main categories, some of which emphasize the organizational context in which training takes place.

Feedback

Feedback evaluation provides quality control over the design and delivery of training activities. Feedback to the participants during training will be an essential part of the learning process. Timely feedback to the trainers about the effectiveness of particular methods and about the achievement of the objectives set for the programme will help in the development of the programme currently being run and those planned for future occasions. The information which needs to be collected for feedback evaluation is:

- the extent to which the objectives are being or have been met
- before and after measures of levels of knowledge, concepts used, skills, attitudes and behaviour
- sufficient detail about content to be able to estimate the effectiveness of each topic covered during the learning event and each learning situation
- evidence of transfer of learning back to the workplace
- some identification of those for whom the programme was of most and of least benefit, so that the target population can be more closely defined.

The main purpose of what we are calling feedback evaluation is the development of learning situations and training programmes to improve what is being offered. There is a secondary aspect, as identifying what is good and what is not so good improves the professional ability of members of the training department. Reports based on feedback evaluation are intended to be *useful* to the trainers (or the training department). If this is to be achieved, the trainers must accept the report as valid and this probably means that they need to be involved in the collection of the data. Feedback reports are particularly useful for the first two or three runs of an activity.

Control

Control evaluation relates training policy and practice to organizational goals. There could also be a concern for the value to the organization of the contribution of the training function, as well as its costs. Careful control evaluation might also answer questions like, 'Will a main focus on training give a better solution to the problem than restructuring the department or redesigning some of the jobs?' The information required for control evaluation is therefore:

- that required for feedback (as listed above)
- some measures of the worth of the output of the training to the organization
- some measures of cost
- some attempt at a comparative study of different combinations of methods for tackling the problem.

Control evaluation is quite close to the left-hand side of the scales in Figure 1. It is something that an organization might require of a training manager or might impose through the creation of a group which is responsible for evaluating but is not part of the training function—an evaluation or monitoring cell. Reports based on control evaluation are intended to supply managers with information which will help them to make decisions. Such reports are usually required when there is some anxiety about whether a particular training activity is meeting its objectives. In some large organizations, reports are required as a matter of course so that the centre can monitor devolved activities.

Research

Research evaluation seeks to add to knowledge of training principles and practice in a way which will have more general application than feedback evaluation. Studies of ways in which people learn or studies of factors which facilitate transfer would be examples. Research evaluation can also serve to improve the techniques available for other purposes like feedback, control and intervention.

Research evaluation is particularly concerned with issues of validity, of which there are two types. Internal validity may be defined as the extent to which particular conclusions may justly be drawn from the data. The data should be derived from a carefully controlled situation with good experimental design so that alternative explanations can be ruled out. External validity is defined as the extent to which conclusions drawn from the experimental situation may be generalizable to other situations.

Research evaluation into training within organizations is particularly difficult, as there is seldom the opportunity to set up a well-designed project with true control groups and time series of observations. If there is no true control group, threats to internal validity will include the following:

- Trends in the organization which produce increased levels of performance through factors which have nothing to do with the programme
- Some people are more likely to volunteer for a programme than others
- People tend to improve with experience whether or not they are trained (Rossi and Freeman, 1989).

Sometimes this can be overcome by using a time series and multiple baselines. Figure 1.2 shows the performance of four groups (say, all of the first line managers) being assessed at 10 intervals (say, monthly production figures). The managers are allocated to training groups in some random fashion and are trained at different times—group A between t1 and t2, group B between t3 and t4 and so on. Each group has its own baseline performance and it is hoped that this will rise as a result of the training intervention.

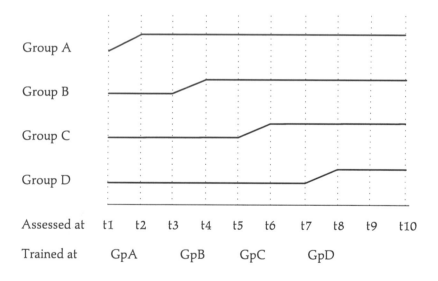

Figure 1.2   *A time series with multiple baselines*

The intention is to discover whether there is a sustained rise in productivity from t2 with group A, t4 with group B, t6 with group C and t8 with group D. The groups provide their own controls as they are trained at different times. It is not difficult to understand why there are so few examples of evaluations carried out as true experiments in the literature. Perhaps the best collection is the set of studies reported by Boruch, McSweeney and Soderstrom (1978). In the last 10 years people seem to have been much less interested in evaluation as science and more interested in evaluation as an intervention.

Intervention

It is probably an illusion to believe that the process of evaluation is the application of some objective measuring instrument external to and independent of the programme being evaluated. The evaluation will almost inevitably affect the way in which the programme is viewed and can be used to redefine the sharing of responsibility for the learning between the trainers, trainees and employing managers. Planned intervention through evaluation can:

- involve the line manager in the pre-post-measurement
- involve the line manager in the extension of training after the event, by debriefing and helping with the implementation of the action plan
- change the way in which the employing managers select and brief people before the learning event
- cause the training department to rethink the deployment of trainers to functions within the organization and strengthen the liaison role.

It can thus be a powerful method of intervening into the human resource procedures within an organization.

The organizational change literature includes many interesting descriptions of the ways in which consultants have changed the ways in which things are done in organizations merely by being present. Perhaps the best known of these is the so-called Hawthorne studies, where the presence of researchers, who were interested in the workforce and what they were doing, had the effect of increasing the volume of work. I recently had a similar experience in a large UK industrial organization. We (the Centre for Training and Evaluation Studies) were asked in as consultants to the central personnel services who were trying to persuade the various regional training groups to evaluate their training. Our contract implied that we were to advise on methods by which the organization could evaluate various types of training. It rapidly emerged that we were making an important contribution by simply going into the various regions around the country and talking about evaluation and its relationship to organizational effectiveness. The informal communications network of regional training managers began to buzz with questions about evaluation and individual managers began to ask themselves questions which they had not asked before. They also became convinced that head office considered the issue to be important (otherwise why would they hire an external consultant?). A number of evaluative studies were started with no more input from us than a request for a date to talk to the regional training manager.

For some, this contention that the evaluation is an intervention in its own right suggests that the process is unscientific and therefore unsatisfactory. However, as Cronbach (1982) pointed out, the purpose of evaluation usually differs from that of scientific investigations. Scientific studies attempt to reach a set of research standards which will be judged by academic peers. Evaluations are designed to recognize the interests of sponsors and stakeholders and their purpose is to provide as much useful information as possible. The standards against which an evaluation might be judged would include the quality of its contribution to the development or implementation of the intervention.

Power games

Perhaps all information is potentially powerful, but certainly evaluative information about training events can be used within the organization in a political way. As it is probably not possible to avoid these power games, perhaps it is not desirable to aim to do so. An evaluator should be aware of these processes and their likely effects. At the very least, the evaluator should ensure that the evidence which is available to be used in this way is based upon a sound study and reliable data.

It is not always possible to prevent the unrepresentative selection of data and thus distorted pictures. For instance, people who would be described as 'negativists' by Randall (1960) make up their minds on anecdotal evidence and are by no means rare. For instance, much of the bad press which sensitivity training received was at the level of 'Did you hear about what happened on the ... programme last week?' A well-founded evaluation study could counter this kind of destructive process.

2 Approaches to evaluation

Goal-based evaluation

Evaluation in its modern form has developed from attempts to improve the educational process, particularly that in the United States. Measurement and assessment of people became popular at about the same time as scientific management, and school officials began to see the possibility of applying these concepts to school improvement.

The most influential early work was that of Tyler, who was appointed in 1932 to be the research director to the eight-year study which was intended to compare the value of progressive high-school curricula with more conventional ones. Tyler's main contribution was to insist that the curricula needed to be organized by the use of objectives. Objectives were seen as being critical because they were the basis for planning, for guiding the instruction and for the preparation of test and assessment procedures. They were also the basis on which a systematic evaluation of a programme could be designed. As he put it (1950, page 69):

The process of evaluation is essentially the process of determining to what extent the educational objectives are actually being realised ... However, since educational objectives are essentially changes in human beings, that is, the objectives aimed at are to produce certain desirable changes in the behaviour patterns of the students, then evaluation is the process for determining the degree to which these changes in behaviour are actually taking place.

The process of evaluation proposed by Tyler had a number of phases as follows:

1 Collect, from as wide a consultation as possible, a pool of objectives which might be related to the curriculum.
2 Screen the objectives carefully to select a subset which covers the desirable changes.
3 Express these objectives in terms of the student behaviours which are expected.
4 Develop instruments for testing each objective. These must meet acceptable standards of objectivity, reliability and validity.
5 Apply the instruments before and after learning experiences.
6 Examine the results to discover strengths and weaknesses in the curriculum.

7 Develop hypotheses about reasons for weaknesses and attempt to rectify these.

8 Modify the curriculum and recycle the process.

Tyler's approach was a distinct advance over existing assessment systems which were based on judgements about the progress of individual students. These judgements were usually based upon examination results and teachers' impressions of classroom work, but there was little attempt to standardize these in such a way that sound comparisons between programmes could be drawn. Educational staff understood the rationale of Tyler's process and valued the way in which it made explicit what it was that they were trying to do.

Training in organizations took some time to catch up with educational theory. It was not until the late 1960s and early 1970s that organizations started to control the quality of training by setting training objectives. Two distinct strands can be identified:

1 The behavioural objectives approach which developed from programmed instruction.

2 Variations on the theme of setting goals to be achieved within the training, after the training activity and longer term.

The behavioural objectives approach is associated with the work of Mager (1962), but the principles are based upon the work of Skinner (1954). This approach advocates the control of training by the setting of objectives which specify performances which can be demonstrated, conditions under which these performances will be tested and the standards which will be acceptable. The trainees are offered these detailed objectives as goals and evaluation is a matter of adding up the numbers attained by individuals and groups.

A goal-based strategy for controlling and evaluating training was adopted by the British Army in 1968. The skills required for successful performance of each of the Army employments were analysed and recorded as behavioural objectives. Training for each 'employment' (the word essentially means 'technical trade') was then designed to meet these objectives. The job analyses showed that some objectives were only necessary for more experienced tradesmen and thus it was possible to structure the training courses at a number of levels (usually three). The process of defining the trade levels in terms of behavioural objectives required a great deal of effort, but it proved to be very successful in improving the effectiveness and efficiency of the training. The main reasons for this success were:

● The objectives were based upon performance derived from the initial analysis of the job and there was no problem in transferring the training.

- Making explicit what the training objectives were removed a good deal of training which had previously been given on the basis of the trainers' ideas of what might be useful.
- The use of the objectives directed the attention of the trainees to what was considered important and allowed them to set learning goals for themselves. Research on adult motivation suggests that this is a sound procedure (see, for instance, Locke and Latham, 1990) which is likely to improve performance.

Courses where technicians were improving their qualifications and thus their earning power, and where they were given a set of behavioural objectives which specified what was required of them, were quite different in nature from the old, instructor-led, programmes. The role of the trainers became one of providing a resource to supply help when asked. The trainees took on much of the responsibility and actually trained themselves. There were some problems with this for trainers who were technical experts. Many of them had enjoyed demonstrating their skills and felt that their talents were not being used properly in the newer, more learner-centred form of training.

An example of a behavioural training objective is given in Figure 2.1. Some feel that such objectives are trivial and cannot capture the richness of the job context. This may be true, but, as can be seen by the example, they offer a comprehensive method for describing what a procedure is, when it is appropriate and when it is inappropriate. A large portion of many jobs can be described at this procedural level, as we will discover when considering how to measure changes in knowledge (page 73) and changes in levels of skills (page 81).

The objective also contains a clear statement of how achievement will be measured, and this greatly simplifies the evaluation. Evaluation becomes an integral part of the training process, as trainees are continually involved in a cycle testing achievement, target setting, learning and re-testing.

A later development in the use of objectives to control training has been to specify the expected outcomes as objectives at a number of levels. The first important contribution to this approach was that of Kirkpatrick (1959), who argued that objectives should be set for the reactions of the trainees to the programme, for learning at the end of the programme, for changed behaviour in the job and for ultimate changes in organizational effectiveness. Others followed this general framework, but offered rather different categories. Figure 2.2 is an attempt to cross-classify the better known approaches. The framework in the columns on the left is a commonsense chronological one, based upon the cycle of learning during training and then applying this in the workplace.

Training Objective No. ....

1 Performance:
   Overtake a moving vehicle
2 Test conditions:
   (a) In any vehicle less than 3 tons unladen weight
   (b) On a public road
   (c) In daylight
   (d) Accompanied by the examiner
3 Test standards:
   (a) Safely, without danger or inconvenience to other
        road users
   (b) Smoothly
   (c) In the appropriate gear for the conditions and
        speeds
   (d) Judge distances, gaps and relative speeds adequately
   (e) Carry out correct sequences as in para 4(a) below
4 Learning points:
   (a) Sequence of action by driver
             (i)   Check mirrors
             (ii)   Signal
             (iii) Select correct gear
             (iv)   Check mirrors
             (v)   Pull out if clear ahead
             (vi)   Cancel signal
             (vii) Overtake
             (viii) Signal intention of coming in
             (ix)   Resume correct road position when safe to
                    do so
             (x)   Cancel signal
             (xi)   Change into top gear (if necessary)
   (b) Restrictions on overtaking
             (i)   Narrow road, bends
             (ii)   Power/size of own vehicle
             (iii) Double white lines
             (iv)   Brows of hills
             (v)   Urban areas—pedestrian crossings, junctions,
                    parked vehicles, etc. (see Highway Code)
             (vi)   Speed limits not to be exceeded
   (c) Overtaking on the left
             (i)   When turning left, vehicle in front turning
                    right, one-way streets
             (ii)   Explain 'filtering'

Figure 2.1   *A behavioural training objective*

The most comprehensive of these frameworks is that offered by
Hamblin (1974). He argues that learning should, as far as possible, be
evaluated in terms of pre-defined objectives. He differs from the
behavioural objectives school in acknowledging that there may be
situations when it is neither desirable nor possible to define the

Areas	Components	Kirkpatrick (1959)	Warr, Bird Rackham (1970)	Glossary (1971)	Hamblin (1974)
Within the training	• Judgements of the quality of trainees' experiences • Feedback to trainees about learning	Reactions	Reactions		Reactions
	• Measures of gain or change • Feedback to trainers about methods	Learning	Immediate	Internal validation	Learning
At the job after training	• Relevance of the learning goals • Measures of use of learning or change of behaviour • Retrospective feedback to trainers	Behaviour	Intermediate	External validation	Job behaviour
Organizational effectiveness	• Measures of change in organizational performance • Implementation of individual/action plans or projects	Results	Ultimate	Evaluation	Organization
Social or cultural values	• Measures of social cost and benefits • Human resources accounting			Evaluation	Ultimate Ultimate

Figure 2.2 *Levels at which objectives can be set*

objectives in detail. The five levels of evaluation are linked by a cause and effect chain:

	Training
leads to	*Reactions*
which lead to	*Learning*
which leads to	*Changes in behaviour*
which lead to	*Changes in the organization*
which lead to	*Change in the achievement of ultimate goals*

My experience as an evaluator indicates that many courses are monitored only at the reactions level and that the main objective is that the trainees should enjoy themselves. Hamblin argues that the reactions measured during and at the end of the programme should meet prespecified objectives which indicate attitude change rather than just enjoyment. Trainers should be specifying in what ways they are hoping that the trainees will react.

Learning, which is defined as 'acquiring the ability to behave in new kinds of ways', should be evaluated against job behaviours of the trainees, and job behaviour objectives should be descriptive of what successful trainees are expected to do when back in post. The expected changes in job behaviour should be linked with changes in effectiveness of the organization, but Hamblin accepts that this is often an assumption. This problem can often be solved by setting objectives for changes lower down, in parts of the organization where criteria of organizational effectiveness can be more precisely defined (see pages 116–122).

Ultimate goals are likely to be commercial in private sector organizations, but in organizations like hospitals or schools the quality of the service itself may form the ultimate goal. Objectives may consequently be product-orientated in the former and process-orientated in the latter.

The strategy which Hamblin is recommending is to select the level at which evaluation is required and then write down the objectives to be achieved at that level and at levels below it. The effects of training can then be evaluated up to that level by assessing the extent to which the pre-set objectives have been achieved. The chain can break down between any two levels, for instance, 'changes in the organization' which are attributable to the training programme will not occur if there are no 'changes in behaviour'.

In practice, few seem to carry goal-based evaluation beyond asking the participants whether they have achieved the objectives set. This will be discussed in the section on measuring reactions as a means of assessing attitude change (page 92). The Alliger and Janak (1989) survey found that good reactions did not predict learning or changed behaviour any better than poor reactions. They also found that the mean correlation between learning and behaviour was 0.13 and that between behaviour and organizational results was 0.19. This implies that the prediction of the higher level from the lower one will, on average, not account for more than 4 *per cent* of the variance. I would argue that these results mean that, if it is necessary to carry out an evaluation, this should be done at all four levels because the different levels are providing different kinds of evidence.

The setting of learning objectives is also to be recommended for on-job development and activities other than off-job courses. The developing employee and the supervisor (perhaps assisted by a member of the training department) analyse the possibilities for learning within the tasks to be done over (say) the next six months. A learning contract is then drawn up which specifies some four to six objectives to be

Objectives set	Strategy for achieving the objectives	Criteria and means of evaluating progress
Objective 1	How you intend to do it	How you intend to measure achievement
Objective 2		
Objective 3		
etc.		
etc.		
Date:	Signed:	Signed:

Figure 2.3 *A learning contract*

achieved during the period. A simple format for the contract is given in Figure 2.3.

The process of developing this contract and evaluating progress is a form of positive performance management combined with personal development and is therefore likely to affect all three aspects of performance in the equation:

Performance = (some function of) Ability × Motivation × Opportunity

The critical aspect of the contract, for evaluative purposes, is the precision with which the criteria are defined.

The logic of the goal-based approach is compelling. Deciding what training is intended to achieve, pre-setting objectives to specify what effects should be seen and then evaluating whether they have been achieved is a sound way to ensure effective training. In practice it is often difficult to produce clear linkages between training content and job tasks, especially in management training. Although it is also difficult to link training objectives to organizational goals, we would support Hamblin in the view that it is worth trying.

The philosophy underlying goal-based approaches is scientific, and the implication is that some form of experimental design will be necessary to answer the questions:

- Have the expected changes occurred? (i.e. is there a significant pre-post-difference?)
- Are the changes attributable to the programme? (i.e. has the data collection process high internal validity?)
- Are the changes likely to occur with other groups? (i.e. is there some degree of external validity?)

The simple design which is most widely used is:

Train   then   Test

Testing takes the form of assessing levels of knowledge, skills and attitudes by actual tests, observation and by asking for trainees' opinions. Opinions of supervisors may also be sought.

There are grave problems of internal validity with such a design:

- Without a pre-test we don't actually know whether there has been a change
- Without some form of control group we don't know if the change identified is attributable to the programme.

A design which overcomes many of the problems of internal validity is:

Group A   pre-test   train   post-test

Group B   pre-test   –   post-test

where the two groups are matched for levels of experience, ability, etc. This is, of course, standard laboratory procedure, but it is very difficult to arrange in an organization.

There is a further problem of deciding whose goals will form the basis for the evaluation—the trainers'?, the participants'?, the managers of the participants?

Suppose that a company introduces a new product and product knowledge programmes are planned:

- **The trainers will have objectives for trying to impart new product knowledge and techniques for using that knowledge in as efficient a way as possible, given the constraints on time.**
- **Sales people attending the programme (or working through the distance learning material) will be hoping to learn something which will assist them to get orders for the new product.**
- **Sales managers will have objectives of reaching targets and obtaining new markets.**
- **The senior management will have the intention of obtaining sales volume which matches the potential product volume and which will secure a healthy share of the market.**

Against whose objectives should the programme be evaluated?

The problem is one which has attracted much recent attention in organizational psychology. Is an organization a group of people with shared goals and common purpose? The logic of goal-based evaluation implies this. An alternative view, which recognizes the political aspect of organizations, is that organizations are made up of groups of people who have different goals.

Responsive evaluation

Goal-based evaluation has lost ground during the last 20 years because of the growing conviction that evaluation is actually a political process and that the various values held in society are not represented by an evaluative process which implies that a high degree of consensus is possible.

The term 'responsive evaluation' was first used by Stake (1975) to describe a strategy in which the evaluator is less concerned with the objectives of the programme than with its effects in relation to the concerns of interested parties—the 'stakeholders'. These stakeholders will usually fall into three broad classes:

- *Agents*, who produce, use or implement the programme to be evaluated
- *Beneficiaries*, who profit in some way from the use of the programme
- *Victims*, who are negatively affected.

The focus of a responsive evaluation is the interests of these various stakeholders, and these are classified in three ways:

- *Claims* are assertions that a stakeholder may introduce which are favourable to the programme
- *Concerns* are assertions which are unfavourable
- *Issues* are things about which 'reasonable people' disagree.

Different stakeholders will have different claims and concerns. A responsive evaluation seeks to identify these and inform representatives of the main stakeholder groups of the claims and concerns of others. Issues will be identified during this process and these will need further investigation to discover if they are due to lack of information or some deeper cause.

In conducting a responsive evaluation, the evaluator first tries to identify the main clients. For a training programme these are likely to be: the staff organizing the programme, those delivering it, and a sample of those who will be affected by it (participants, their supervisors and more senior line managers). The aim is to gain a sense of their different postures with regard to the programme and the purposes which each group has for the evaluation. Guba and Lincoln (1989) suggest asking each interviewee, 'Do you know of someone who has views which are very different from yours?', and thus building up the sample from those with differing opinions. My experience is that it may be necessary to select the sample more formally (for instance, stratifying by dividing participants into production, finance, marketing and personnel, and then ensuring that the sample includes some of each category) in order to include the full range of points of view. The evaluator then makes personal observations of the programme to get a direct sense of what it is about. He or she has begun to discover the purpose of the programme, both stated and real, and also the concerns that various stakeholders may have. Now the evaluator is in a position to conceptualize the issues and problems which the evaluation should address.

The design of the evaluation takes place next, and it should be noted that this is well into the process of evaluation. It cannot be designed before the evaluator can specify the kinds of data and information which will be needed to satisfy the various issues and concerns. The evaluator selects whichever methods and instruments are most appropriate and collects data. The information collected is organized into themes and the evaluator matches issues and concerns to audiences in deciding what form the report will take (as there may be different reports for different audiences). It is worth noting the interactions implicit in this process; at any stage the evaluator or the sponsor may reformulate what is to be done.

The direction of the evaluation is not fixed at the outset, but readjusted as data become available. There is no natural end point but simply a place convenient for reporting. Given sufficient time and budget, the evaluator could recycle the entire evaluation process as a result of changes in the concerns of the stakeholders' contingent on their receiving their reports.

Parlett and Hamilton (1977) describe a form of evaluation which has some similarities to responsive evaluation and recommend it for educational research. The primary concern of 'illuminative evaluation' is with description and interpretation rather than with measurement and prediction. The suggested method by which to achieve this is 'progressive focusing', which means the systematic reduction of the breadth of the enquiry to give more concentrated attention to the emerging issues. A key value which is apparent in the work of Parlett and Hamilton is that they reject the classical evaluator's stance of seeking an objective truth that is equally relevant to all of the parties in favour of acknowledging the diversity of questions posed by different interest groups.

Legge (1984) also arrives at a position which is quite close to that of responsive evaluation from a quite different route. She discusses the research on evaluation of planned organizational change, and criticizes it on two main grounds. The first of these is that evaluation research which is rigorous enough to be acceptable to an academic is almost always too trivial to be useful to decision makers as the designs are so restrictive that most of the things which are of interest are controlled out. The second is that most of the research is so badly designed that it is unacceptable to an academic because threats to internal validity have not been controlled and there is little confidence in the conclusions drawn. Legge suggests that, rather than attempting evaluation as rigorously controlled research, a 'contingent approach' be adopted. This essentially consists of asking the major stakeholders four major questions:

1 Do you want the proposed change programme to be evaluated?
2 What functions do you wish the evaluation to serve?
3 Which approach (of a number of possible alternatives) best matches the functional requirements of the evaluation exercise?
4 To what extent are constraints on the planning and implementation of the change programme, which will be necessary because of this approach to evaluation, acceptable?

The underlying philosophy of responsive evaluation is very different from that which is based upon scientific enquiry. It is worth while listing some of the assumptions to emphasize this:

● 'Truth' is a matter of consensus among informed people. It does not correspond to an objective reality.
● 'Facts' have no meaning except within some value framework and an evaluation will produce data in which facts and values are inextricably mixed.
● Evaluators are subjective partners with stakeholders in the creation of data. The evaluation is a joint, collaborative process which results in something being *constructed* rather than *revealed* by the investigation.
● Phenomena can only be understood in the context in which they are studied, so that generalization from an evaluation is unlikely.

As Campbell put it (in Dunnette and Hough, 1992), when writing about applied research:

Experimental validity and statistical power are not so crucial as consensus about the importance of the question, agreement of all parties about the form the research should take, and using pooled observations from the legitimate stakeholders as the basic data.

The emphasis on internal validity in the scientific approach will often imply controlling out key aspects of the context and many organizational variables. This may result in rather simplified information which clients find difficult to use because it does not reflect their perception of organizational reality. The evaluation report will usually be written for the client, who may not be the person who has to implement changes, and this can also lead to problems of utility. The responsive approach involves protracted negotiations with a wide range of stakeholders in constructing the report. It is thus more likely to reflect their reality and be useful for them.

Not many responsive evaluations have been described in the training literature. An example is given here in the hope that it will help to clarify the process and likely outcomes. The training for recruits to police forces in the UK is organized as a series of modules, each expected to build upon the learning gained in those preceding it. Module 1 is a general familiarization with police work by observation within a police force, module 2 is a 10-week basic training course in a district training centre (DTC), module 3 is a five-week attachment to an operational unit where the probationer 'shadows' an experienced constable, module 4 is a five-week course in a district training centre and module 5 is another five-week attachment to an operational unit where the probationer works with a tutor constable. There are other modules, but these do not need to concern us here.

Module 4 is intended to be an opportunity for probationers to reflect on their previous experience and that of others. They are also expected to discuss complex situations where judgement is necessary rather than a simple understanding of the law. There was some doubt about the effectiveness of module 4, and we (the Centre for Training and Evaluation Studies) were asked to assist with the evaluation of it.

As the objectives for the module were not at all clear, or shared between the interested parties, we decided to use a responsive approach. Besides the central quality control committee, our contact client, the main stakeholders, were identified as being: the force training officers who were responsible for the development of all officers in their forces; the senior management of the district training centres who set the climate and, to some extent, the syllabus for modules 2 and 4; the trainers responsible for running module 4; the tutor constables; and the probationers themselves. We visited all the district training centres and interviewed a sample of each of the stakeholder groups listed above. All were asked what *claims* they made for module 4 and what their *concerns* were. These were summarized, and *issues*, where there was considerable disagreement, were identified. The report of this part of the evaluation was circulated among the stakeholders to show what consensus had been found and what issues had been identified.

It was suggested in the preliminary report that the evaluation should proceed by collecting more evidence on the five major *issues*. This report was circulated in the September before the November meeting of the quality control committee which was to agree terms of reference for the further evaluation.

It was clear at this meeting that the report was already out of date. Two of the issues where further investigation had been suggested were:

'Are the trainers able to run module 4 in the way intended by the designers?'

'Is the prevailing culture within DTCs conducive to achieving the objectives of module 4?'

By the November meeting, many of the senior managers of the DTCs had reviewed the training and tasking of their module 4 trainers. Some had also taken steps to alter the climate of the DTC, to make it more conducive to reflective study based upon trainee-centred learning.

It should be clear from this example that, in a responsive evaluation, the evaluator becomes part of the intervention. The process is like action learning, where there is a cycle of data collection and action based upon these data. It is not an objective, non-interventionist, scientific approach. In our example there was a second stage of collecting data to gain further understanding of the issues identified. At the same time, however, redesigned module 4 courses were being run as pilots in two of the DTCs. The evaluation had thus become part of the development of module 4, and both were happening together, each feeding off the other. This is not at all like the process of trying to discover to what extent pre-set objectives have been achieved, submitting a report and hoping that changes will be made.

Responsive evaluation is gaining ground as the most favoured method for evaluating educational and social programmes in the USA. It has obvious strengths as a procedure for evaluating training and development activities within organizations because it attempts to take into account the interests of various groups rather than just the sponsors of the programme. It also has a rationale for collecting information—the needs of the various stakeholders.

Systematic evaluation

The title suggests that the strategy of systematic evaluation will be the analysis of the whole system and the relationships between sub-systems. The purpose of such an analysis would be to improve the interfaces between the sub-systems in such a way as to increase the effectiveness of the system. That is what 'systems approaches' set out to do. The most comprehensive description of the strategy of systematic evaluation is to be found in the book by Rossi and Freeman (1989). What one discovers by reading this is that the main questions which this strategy actually sets out to answer are:

- Is the programme reaching the target population?
- Is it effective?
- How much does it cost?
- Is it cost-effective?

These are questions posed by policy makers who are interested in 'the facts' and not in opinions, and the problems with this approach are implicit in the collection of this kind of 'hard' data. The first question will be answered by defining the size of the target population and working out the proportion who have attended, i.e. 'reaching' is being defined in terms of attendance rather than useful learning. One might argue that defining 'reaching' in this way makes it a trivial criterion. 'Effectiveness' is difficult to measure in terms which satisfy those who want simple statistics. For instance, much of the work in the public sector in the UK now seems to be evaluated in terms of 'how many' (patients per year, arrests per month, GCSE passes, etc.) rather than the quality of what is being done.

A more productive way of thinking about a systems approach to evaluation is to consider the training department as an organizational sub-system and look at the relationship between the work it is doing and the business plans for the various parts of the organization. A framework like those based upon aspects of organizational effectiveness (pages 114–122) will help in this. The intention would be to evaluate to what extent training was contributing to increased performance against the criteria of effectiveness thought to be key results areas for the particular organizational sub-system. An outline based upon Figure 2.4 would help.

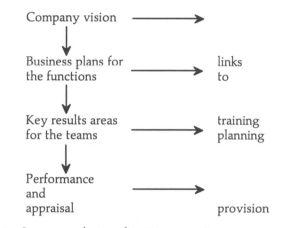

Figure 2.4   *Systems analysis and training provision*

Given our analysis of the training process in Part Two of this book, we might also add some further questions:

- Are the needs which the training is intended to meet defined in criteria which can be measured against aspects of effectiveness?
- Is the learning being designed in such a way that it is likely to transfer, and result in, different work behaviours?

It might also be worth while considering whether the projected benefits outweigh the likely costs.

Quasi-legal approach

Quasi-legal evaluation operates like a court of inquiry. Witnesses are called to testify and submit evidence. Great care is taken to hear a wide range of evidence (opinions, values and beliefs) from the organizers of the programme and the 'users' as well as the accountants. Such an approach has been used to evaluate social programmes, but not, to my knowledge, for formally evaluating training or development activities sponsored by organizations. It might be suitable for such a purpose, provided a sufficiently impartial 'judge' could be found and provided some agreement could be reached about who comprised the key witnesses.

A flawed example of quasi-legal evaluation was reported by Porter and McKibbin (1988). The topic under investigation was the appropriate nature and direction of management education in the USA. A huge amount of information was collected from thousands of stakeholders and was analysed by a small group of professors from business schools.

They reported that business schools were generally very pleased with their contribution (and were using increases in numbers of MBA students as their main criterion of success). Graduates generally felt that the qualification which they had obtained was useful and the courses were worth while. However, the criticism which Mintzberg (1992) and others have made—that the young graduates who now attend MBA courses have never worked in an organization and thus do not understand the sorts of issues which should be the basic discussion material of MBA courses—was not addressed.

A similar problem arose with the Constable and McCormick (1987) report on the demand for and supply of management education and training in the UK. They surveyed 100 suppliers, 100 users and 200 large organizations. One of the findings was that employers and managers wanted training and education processes which were, as far as possible, integrated into working activities. However, the main recommendation of the report was that MBA places should be increased from some 1600 in 1985 to 5000 in 1992 and 10 000 by the year 2000. In my view, professors of business schools are not sufficiently impartial judges for the evaluation of the provision of management training and education.

Pre-programme evaluation

It is not uncommon in training to evaluate, in a rather informal way, a number of possible methods of structuring an activity before it is implemented. Given some information about the prospective target population, the objectives for the programme and the type of learning required, some decision criteria can be established for selecting a training design and the media to support it. Education technology books like Davies (1971) and algorithms like CRAMP (Pearn, 1981) offer a variety of rationales for this selection.

Pre-programme evaluation goes a little further than this and asks whether the procedures being considered are likely to bring about the desired changes. Warr, Bird and Rackham (1970) call this 'input evaluation' and suggest that the following questions should be posed:

- What are the relevant merits of different training techniques?
- Is it feasible to run the training within the organization or will the services of some external agency be needed?
- Does the age or background of the trainees suggest any particular training method?
- How much time is likely to be available for training?

● What were the results last time a similar programme was run?

The organizational change literature on 'institutionalization' and 'routinization' of changes also provides some criteria which are necessary to carry out a pre-programme evaluation. For instance, Goodman and Dean (1982) focus on the factors which affect the persistence of a new policy or procedure which has been introduced as an intended change. They argue that institutionalization is a continuum which starts with knowledge of the change at one end and then goes through 'performance' and 'preference' to reach 'incorporation into norms and values' at the other. In order to assess where individuals and groups fall on this continuum it is necessary to examine five processes:

1 *Socialization*—the extent to which information is transmitted to organizational members about the required behaviours, etc.
2 *Commitment*—whether people are accepting the change by personal choice or by external constraints.
3 *Reward allocation*—the extent to which rewards are related to desired behaviours.
4 *Diffusion*—the extent to which the new form is spreading to other parts of the organization.
5 *Sensing and calibration*—the extent to which feedback information, which can be used to take corrective action, is available.

The culture of the organization interacts with these five processes, and it is against this that we might be able to predict whether or not the change is likely to be accepted into organizational procedures and thus survive in the longer term. If, for each of the five processes above, we ask (say) a representative steering committee to estimate 'The extent to which it is likely that . . .', this should give an evaluation of the likely success of the programme before it is implemented. It should also alert the designers to some of the key issues which need to be addressed if good transfer is to be achieved.

3 Issues in evaluation

Objectivity of evaluation

Within all of these approaches it is possible to use different levels of analysis—individual, work groups, departments, inter-departments or overall organization. Usually it is necessary to attempt some synthesis of these levels when producing a balanced report. It should be obvious from this and from a consideration of the various strategies available that the evaluation will never produce the truth. The objectives approach will lead to the collection of relatively 'hard' data which can be reliably measured, but the evaluators will hold values which determine which objectives will be investigated and what evidence will be acceptable. Systematic evaluation will also produce 'hard' data, but it has similar problems to the goal-based approach. The other approaches are more subjective in their methods of collecting data, but attempt to get at a wider 'truth'.

The objectivity within an evaluation comes from a conviction that if someone else had carried out the study he or she would have come to similar conclusions. As Professor Alec Rodger (the founder of the Occupational Psychology Department at Birkbeck College, University of London) used to say: 'A study should be technically sound, administratively convenient and politically defensible.' The evaluation will rarely be objective in the scientific sense of a passive observation of events. This is only possible when unobtrusive measures are being used (things like statistics on absence, or levels of production, or sales volume per number of visits). An evaluation will usually become part of the training process as the presence of the evaluator in a part of the organization will, to some extent, change the perceptions of some of the people about some of the changes and some of the objectives of the training activity.

Presenting an evaluation report

The final stage of most evaluations will be the presentation of the report. The extent to which this will be accepted and acted upon will depend to a large extent on what took place at the beginning of the study. It is crucial to identify the major stakeholders and to try to discover what agendas they have. Sensitivity to the conflicting aims and interests can be enhanced by discussing with a number of stakeholders what data should be collected. Many of those who have a long-term interest in the programme will have strong views on the desired outcomes of the study. It is essential to keep such people informed during the evaluation and to involve them in key decisions if they are to 'own' and therefore act on the results. This is not to imply that the evaluator must produce the findings which they are expecting; rather that their views must be incorporated and they must be kept informed. It is, of course, also essential to establish that the people receiving the report have the power to implement the changes being suggested.

One way of overcoming some of the problems in presenting the report is to discover what kind of report the major stakeholders expect. At the beginning of this part of the book, you were asked to decide what it was that you meant by evaluation. Making a decision on each of the scales in Figure 1 makes explicit what kind of process evaluation is thought to be. I suggest that, before embarking on an evaluation, you ask the major stakeholders to fill in a set of attitude scales like those in Figure 1. You will then know what kind of data they think you ought to collect and something about how they expect you to present it. That should at least alert you to some of the problems if their views are very different from your own. In most cases I think that it will also assist the process of putting the case and helping them to make changes.

The nature of the report will, of course, reflect the purpose for which it is written, but generally it will contain most of the following sections:

1 A *summary*, which is intended for those who will not have time to read the full report. Care should be taken to ensure that this is a balanced extract, as many people will not read (or remember) the supporting arguments in the main body of the report.
2 A statement of the *purpose* of the evaluation and how it was designed to meet that purpose.
3 A description of the *methods* used for data collection and a summary of the findings.
4 A summary of *costs*.
5 The *results* expressed in terms of increased individual and organizational benefits.
6 *Conclusions* drawn from the previous sections. These may sometimes be recommendations if the purpose of the evaluation requires these.

The way in which the findings are communicated during the study will depend upon organizational style. Some organizations prefer written memoranda, but in many the important decisions are actually made in face-to-face discussions. Discussion of what is emerging from the data often leads to a greater sense of shared responsibility and thus a willingness to accept the results as being valid. The presentation of the report itself is not the time to 'defend'. If there is some bad news, those concerned should be aware of it before the presentation. At the very least, this allows them to say that they are aware of some problems and have started to do something about them, rather than provoking a defensive reaction.

An evaluation report will usually be a part of a change process and it is helpful to consider the method of change which is to be used. The literature on planned organizational change can help here, as a number of models for this process have been described.

One possible method is the *research, development and dissemination* model (Havelock, 1969). In this the research leads to a report which contains conclusions for further development. This report is widely circulated and the information so disseminated is acted on by the target audience. This model assumes that the recipients of the report are essentially passive consumers and that they are rational. They will then agree that the study is valid, accept its conclusions, see the importance of the changes and be willing to make them. This is a very popular method in large organizations, but it often has little effect because one or more of the assumptions is not justified.

A second possibility is the *social interaction model* (Havelock, 1969). This is more sensitive to the relationships and processes which are involved in the dissemination phase. The users are seen as holding a variety of positions and as being likely to adopt attitudes and behaviour which vary with their reference group. This model implies that it is necessary to make face-to-face contacts with the different audiences and that the process is nearer one of negotiation than one of simple dissemination of information.

A third plausible method is the *planned change model* (Sashkin, Morris and Horst, 1973). Here data collection and research is shared between the change agent and the client. Information is considered useful only if it leads to action. The assumption is that change occurs through a continuous process of data generation, planning and implementation. The changes which are introduced need to be supported and 'routinized' if they are to be fully utilized.

The purpose of the evaluation will vary and the process will differ in different organizations. What I am suggesting is that you should think about the process and ask yourself the following questions:

- Are you intending to produce conclusions or achieve change?
- What sort of target audience have you? Are they relatively passive and likely to accept the changes? Do the changes need to be negotiated?
- When do you withdraw from the scene? Should you continue to be involved as a change agent would be until the changes have become part of the routine?

Whatever method is adopted, a successful presentation of a report should result in action planning by the recipients. An effective report must contain information which the recipients will find meaningful as they are unlikely to introduce changes if they cannot understand the data or do not find them relevant to their problems. The information should also have some impact so that it can energize some change and be a stimulus for further action or investigation. This may often mean a clear statement that something is wrong and that it needs attention. It may also mean that suggestions about how to start changing the *status quo* will be necessary in order to overcome inertia. It is worth emphasizing again that the report should be presented to those who have the ability to make the necessary changes.

The likelihood of evaluations being used depends upon evaluators' recognition that the key determinants of their utilization are the interpersonal and political contexts in which the evaluations are undertaken (Rossi and Freeman, 1989, page 421).

Utilization of findings

An evaluation is carried out to meet a purpose, and one might argue that the work is only worth while if the findings are used. Van de Vall and Bolas (1981) investigated the extent to which findings from evaluations were used. They found that there was a higher rate of utilization for findings produced by internal researchers than for externals. The key variable was thought to be the higher rate of communication between the internals and policy makers.

The review by Leviton and Hughes (1981) suggested four aspects which might have an important effect on utilization:

1 Relevance of the findings to decisions which need to be made.
2 Communication between researchers and users.
3 Plausibility of the research results.
4 User involvement in the evaluation.

Solomon and Shortell (1981) offer guidelines for increasing the likelihood of utilization:

1 Understand the cognitive style of the decision makers (for instance, there is no point in presenting complex statistical analysis to a politician, but it might be necessary if you are trying to convince a scientist).
2 Oral presentations and answering questions will usually be more appropriate than long papers.
3 Wide participation in the design process is necessary to increase sensitivity to the interests of various stakeholders.

These three studies on utilization emphasize a point made earlier—that however careful and scientific the collection of data, it is often useful to think of evaluation as a political process. As Patton's (1978) research has shown, scientific validity (whether other researchers think that the study accords with sound scientific principles) is often far less important than face validity (for instance, whether the information sources are thought to be reliable) when estimating the degree to which evaluative findings will be used.

Ethical issues

One aspect of this political flavour of evaluation is that ethical issues are often raised. Morris and Cohn (1993) reported the findings of a survey of 456 professional evaluators who were asked whether they had encountered any ethical problems in their work. If the answer to this question was 'yes', each respondent was asked to describe the three most frequent and the one most serious problem. Problems rated as 'frequent' included:

- Stakeholder had already decided what the findings should be (reported by 55 per cent of the respondents)
- Evaluator discovers something that is illegal, unethical or dangerous (14 per cent)
- Evaluator pressured by stakeholder to violate confidentiality (26 per cent)
- Evaluator pressured by stakeholder to alter presentation or findings (62 per cent)
- Findings suppressed or ignored (32 per cent)
- Findings used to punish the evaluator (10 per cent)
- Findings used to punish someone else (16 per cent).

There was also the interesting finding that those who had experienced ethical problems were mainly external evaluators. Those who spent the majority of their time on internal evaluations tended to report not having to face ethical problems. It seems unlikely that internal evaluations involve fewer ethical problems than external ones, and Morris and Cohn (1993) argue that it is more likely that internals are so close to the problems (and the stakeholders) that they do not recognize the ethical issues.

Summary

Evaluation, as it has been described here, is a process of collecting information. The information to be collected is that thought necessary to meet a particular purpose. It is not economic and, indeed, not feasible to evaluate something from all perspectives. Definitions which imply that evaluation is 'The assessment of the total value ... in social as well as financial terms' (*Glossary of Training Terms*, 1981) actually make it impossible ever to evaluate. It is therefore important, at the outset, to decide why the evaluation is being carried out.

The information may be needed for the development of learning activities or programmes, quality control, assessing the return on investment, identifying further training needs or relating training policy to organizational goals. The *why* will determine what information needs to be collected and this, in turn, will affect the decision about which approach is most likely to meet the purpose. The purpose may also include intervening in organizational processes, particularly where changes in procedures are intended.

Goal-based approaches are recommended where fairly precise goals, objectives and targets have been identified and where these are widely accepted. Evaluation using a goal-based strategy is, essentially, trying to discover if changes are *caused* by the intervention. It is therefore necessary to have pre-intervention measures as a baseline against which to measure change and some control over organizational variables which might also cause the changes which are expected.

Responsive, constructivist approaches are recommended where there is likely to be considerable variation in what the objectives of a programme are thought to be. Responsive approaches involve the stakeholders in the collection of data and are a form of action research. The intention is not to attribute causality, but to gain a sense of the value of the programme seen from a number of different perspectives. They are thus much more overtly political than goal-based approaches.

Presenting an evaluation report often implies asking for changes to be made. This is *always* a political activity, and thought must be given to how it is done and how to involve those who will be making the changes. The extent to which evaluation findings will be used will depend upon how sensitive the process has been to the interests of the various stakeholders. The level of communication between those who have collected the data and those who (it is hoped) will use them may be the crucial variable.

PART TWO

Evaluating the training process

Introduction

The main thrust of this part of the book is that the processes by which training is designed and delivered can be evaluated against examples of good practice. Any process is made up of steps and, if it is systematic, each of these will arise logically from the model on which it is based. It is therefore worth while starting at this basic level and looking at the underlying model of any training activity. Models of training have different assumptions and are suitable for different purposes. Some models encourage discourse and assume that useful learning takes place as a result of interaction with others who have greater or, perhaps, different experience. Some are based on the principle that successful job performance is judged by the assessment of skills levels and thus the function of training becomes to improve individual skills. Other models focus on improved effectiveness in the organizational context. It must surely be worth considering whether the model on which a training activity is based is actually consistent with the purpose. Examination of the literature and experience of practice suggests that very few trainers actually do this.

Training needs can be identified at both organizational and individual levels. If the training is to be embedded in an organizational context, it would seem relevant for the identification process to take account of both levels and to try to balance the need for development of individuals with the requirements of the organization. Many trainers feel that their contribution is at the individual level. I believe that they will have more influence within the organization, and make a greater contribution to its well-being, if they also consider the higher level.

The way in which trainees are selected, and the extent to which they as individuals are likely to be able to use the new skills or knowledge in their work, are clearly crucial to the success of the programme in terms of improved organizational effectiveness. Selecting trainees on a 'remedial' basis, because they are judged to lack certain skills, will logically lead to certain kinds of training process. Developmental activities should imply quite different processes, with more emphasis on work-based assignments and less on off-job courses.

The delivery of the programme itself is usually assessed against criteria of 'how well it went' seen from the perspective of the trainees as well as the tutors. There are more sophisticated ways of looking at the process during the programme, and these are worth considering as they add information to the basic, reaction, level of assessment.

If the things learned during the training are to result in different ways of doing the job, then some thought must be given to the transfer process. The process of transfer can start in the training, with the use of action planning and focusing on the utility of the learning, but it is often the case that, for effective transfer, the supervisor or line manager will need to be involved. The model which many trainers are using precludes their close contact with line managers and thus their ability to influence the quality of the transfer. Other models require close contact with line managers and, where transfer of training is thought to be a problem, these might be more suitable.

These issues will be discussed one by one, and then, at the end of this part of the book, an attempt will be made to integrate them into a strategy for evaluating by examining processes.

4 Models of training

The individual training model

Training of individuals has its origin in craft apprenticeships, where a young person learned, over a period of some years, to imitate the skills of his master. The learning model in use here was an ancient one, with hand–eye skills being learned by the method of demonstration followed by practice followed by further demonstration. Training for trades and technical training in general have been greatly influenced by this tradition of teaching skills to individuals in the belief that they will later find a use for them. The model which is in use here is illustrated in Figure 4.1.

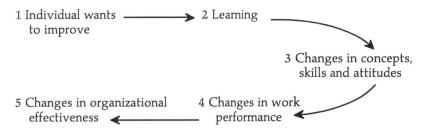

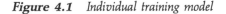

Figure 4.1   *Individual training model*

The focus is on individuals and the process is one of encouraging them to learn something said to be useful and then expecting them to find uses for the learning. This echoes the process of education in our schools and concentrates on only the first two parts of our definition of training. In attempting to evaluate training based on this model, it is sometimes very difficult to identify changes in work performance. With many forms of technical training, where the equipment used in training is very similar to that in the workplace, the changes in skills levels achieved during training will transfer quite easily into the job (provided there is an opportunity to practise them there). The model is, however, being used for other forms of training. Since the 1950s, it has become more and more necessary to train managers and supervisors as well as blue-collar workers. The model shown in Figure 4.1 is inappropriate for this kind of training if the purpose is to change the way in which things are done in the organization rather than to learn well-defined skills. As Katz and Kahn (1978, page 658) point out, attempts to change parts of organizations by using models like this have a 'long history of theoretical inadequacy and practical failure'. The logic of the approach is that, as organizations are made up of individuals, it must be possible to change the organization by changing the members. This is, however, a great simplification of organizational reality. An organization will have objectives, priorities and policies. It will also have a structure and accepted ways of doing things. All of these situational factors will have some effect on shaping the behaviour of members of the organization within their work. Often the 'changed' individual is not able to change these situational factors.

It is worth while investigating this further as it is crucial to an understanding of why training sometimes fails to have any effect. The work context can be represented as an interaction between the situation and the people in it (see Figure 4.2). If this interaction is not as effective as it might be, then changing the people by training might be considered as a way of improving things. However, this will only be successful if the people are sufficiently autonomous to change the interaction and thus the work situation. This might be the case where people are trained to use a piece of equipment like a keyboard or a lathe, but there is no reason to assume that it is the case with the sorts of problems which supervisors face. Other factors influence the alternatives and possible decisions and these factors may be more powerful in determining how the work is done than the skills of the people involved.

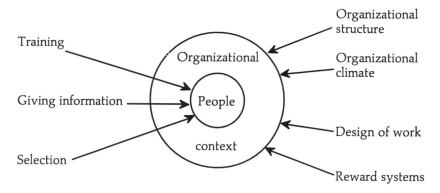

Figure 4.2 *Changing the way the work is done*

Such things as the structure of the organization (who reports to whom, how many levels and whether people can communicate horizontally), the climate (in what spirit people relate to each other, to what extent individuality is valued), the design of the work (the extent to which this is frustrating or stress-inducing), and whether good performance is actually rewarded (by recognition, praise and promotion, as well as financially) will all affect the job situation. In order to achieve behaviour change in the workplace, it will often be necessary to change some of these situational factors as well as to change the abilities and attitudes of the people.

A distinction is being drawn here between training and giving information. The latter is a method which is widely used for changing the people side of the interaction. At its most basic this may be feedback on organizational performance and an indication of how far this falls short of expectations, but there are many more sophisticated forms. Some, like management briefings and job induction programmes, are usually funded from the training department budget. It should also be noted that changing the people by selecting different people to fill key appointments, or regrouping people into teams where more cooperation and less conflict is likely, might be a more effective method than training the people who are in the posts.

Increased effectiveness model

We can see that changing the performance of people in the job is rather more complicated than Figure 4.1 would suggest. In order to think this through we need to consider a model which is based on changing effectiveness rather than on educating individuals. If one were to start at the end of the chain in Figure 4.1, with desired changes in effectiveness, try to decide what behaviours would be necessary to achieve these, and then analyse what knowledge, skills and attitudes (KSAs) would be required to underpin these behaviours, a model like that in Figure 4.3 would emerge. At stage 4 in this model, aspects of the job situation other than the skills of the people will be considered, and it may be that changing some of these will achieve the desired improvements without training. If training is then thought to be necessary it is delivered, and the extent to which any learning is useful will be monitored by changes in job performance, not, as is usually the case with the model in Figure 4.1, by changes measured during the training.

This model is much more appropriate for the kind of work where people have some discretion about what they do or the ability to negotiate priorities. It is not necessary to carry out an analysis in this depth if the intention is to transfer simple skills. However, it is no longer the case that most jobs are based upon simple skills; rather, the requirement is for discretion and innovation. Where these are considered necessary, a model which includes organizational aspects will be superior to one based upon individual learning.

Considering the organizational context when using a model like this can have significant benefits. In a study reported by McGarrell (1984), induction training of new employees was redesigned to prepare them for the social context of the job and for the frustrations and

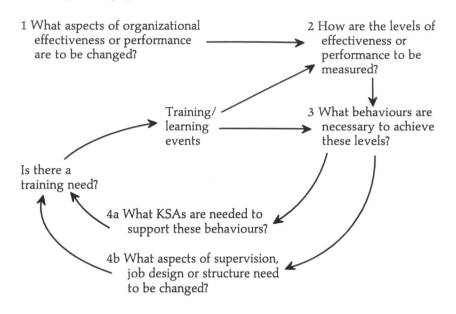

Figure 4.3   *Increased effectiveness model*

opportunities of learning on-the-job. They also learned how their contribution would fit into their part of the organization and into the organization as a whole. The loss of people by leaving during the three-month induction period dropped by 70 per cent and this gave a benefit-to-cost ratio of 8:1.

On the other hand, ignoring the organizational context can be expensive. Sykes (1962) described a training programme in which all 97 supervisors in an organization were trained to be more participative in their management style. The values instilled during training were not those of the management of the organization, and the supervisors were frustrated in their attempts to introduce participative management in the workplace. Within a year, 19 of the supervisors had left and another 25 were actively seeking other employment. The training, although efficient in changing the attitudes of the supervisors, was not effective in contributing to organizational goals.

The training programme described by Sykes was planned using an individual model like that in Figure 4.1. Given the discussion above, is this the most likely model to achieve more participative management in an organization? What assumptions are being made? I would suggest the following:

● the supervisors can learn the skills and procedures
● they will be motivated to learn these off-the-job
● the motivation to use the new procedures will persist when they return to the workplace

- their colleagues, managers and subordinates will allow them, or even encourage them, to use the new procedures
- there will be some external benefit in terms of increased effectiveness in the department to compensate for the extra time spent on participative management
- they will be willing to persist with the new procedures despite disappointments and discouragement.

You will not be surprised to learn that some of these assumptions were not satisfied.

An alternative strategy would be to use a model like that in Figure 4.3. The first question is, 'What changes in effectiveness are expected?', followed by, 'How will we measure these changes?' The answers would probably be given in terms of behaviours like:

- To what extent are work tasks and targets set jointly?
- How often is progress towards the targets jointly reviewed?
- To what extent is responsibility and authority delegated?
- How often are subordinates asked about their views on work, or asked to suggest new ways in which things could be done?
- Is the manager available and spending time with subordinates when needed?
- Does the manager know when individuals have problems? Is he or she helpful and supportive?

The most likely source of such information is the subordinates, who could be asked to comment on each of these questions using some form of rating scale. It would probably be necessary to allow them anonymity in this. Each supervisor might then have, say, six-monthly feedback of the collated perceptions of his or her subordinates. This feedback, with or without training on topics such as joint target setting, listening or holding team meetings, could help change the management style in the organization to a more participative one.

It should be noted that this model and procedure is profoundly different from that shown in Figure 4.1. The intention is the same—to change the way that individuals work—but now the new behaviours are embedded in the organizational context. In the earlier model they were encouraged in a training context and it was hoped that individuals would apply them in their work. I suggest that you consider these two models as possible ways of changing part of the culture of your organization, say, trying to achieve a more consultative management style. Would training individual managers and supervisors and returning them to an unsuspecting workplace be likely to succeed? Would the procedure suggested by Figure 4.3 be more or less likely to succeed?

Summary

The model of training which is most prevalent has developed from educational practice, where the intention is to teach an individual how to carry out some part of a well-defined job. Where the information and/or skills practice given is closely matched to a job which is not changing, this may be an adequate model. Where it is intended that the training given should help the individual to change the job situation, this model is often not appropriate as it assumes that the individual has sufficient autonomy to change the way in which 'things are done' in part of the organization. If the intention is to change the effectiveness of the individual or of part of the organization, a different model may be more appropriate. This is controlled by measuring changes in criteria of effectiveness rather than by input of hours of tutoring. The model is one of organizational change combined with learning, rather than the more traditional approach of training the individual.

5 Identification of training needs

The accurate identification of the training needs of an organization is crucial to its success and development. However, theory does little to assist those who face this difficult task. It is not simply a matter of deciding on the location, scope and magnitude of the needs. Priorities need to be set and linked to those of other functions within the organization as well as to the goals of the organization as a whole.

Three levels of analysis

The most influential text on training needs analysis is that of McGehee and Thayer (1961). They argue that training needs analysis requires much more than 'armchair cerebration' and suggest analysis at three levels—the organization, the job and the person. Although the needs analysis will usually consist of three distinct investigations, McGehee and Thayer argue that these should be interrelated so that they build on each other to produce a complete training needs statement.

- Analysis at the organizational level is used to determine where training can and should be used. The focus is the total enterprise and the analysis will look, among other things, at the organizational objectives, the short-term business plan, longer-term views on how the environment might change in the next few years, the pool of skills presently available, indices of effectiveness and benchmarking against competitors.
- Analysis at the job level involves collecting data about a particular job or group of jobs. The analysis will determine what standards are required and what knowledge, skills and attitudes are needed in order to achieve these standards.
- Person analysis focuses on how well a particular employee is carrying out the various tasks which are necessary for successful performance.

Organizational analysis

Training and development is a sub-system of the organization and receives inputs from the organization and offers outputs to the organization. If this interaction is to result in increased organizational effectiveness then it is clear that priorities for training needs must be related to organizational goals. This implies that the training plan should be constructed in the same context as the business plan and be closely related to it. Hussey's survey (1985) of British companies suggests that only about a third of them actually do this. Most managers felt that training objectives should be tailored to the individual rather than to corporate needs. Hussey argues that training should not be for the individual in the hope that it will benefit the organization; it should be for the benefit of the organization as this will benefit the individuals in it. Thus, according to Hussey, training objectives, especially those for management development, should be reviewed regularly by top management and particularly whenever a change in direction or emphasis is planned. It appears that, in the USA, the likelihood of this happening is increasing. Bolt's survey (1987) showed that betweeen 1983 and 1986 there was an increase in top management commitment to management training and development and that 'Senior corporate management is expecting the training profession to deliver results and to contribute materially to implementing corporate strategies and achieving business objectives'.

McGehee and Thayer recommend a number of sources of data to support the analysis of needs at the organizational level:

- Organizational goals and objectives will provide targets for the various functions within the organization. Some of these will imply changes in performance standards and these may have training implications.
- The manpower plan will predict gaps caused by retirements, promotions and turnover. This provides a demographic basis for identifying training (and selection) required to fill the gaps.
- The skills pool is an inventory of knowledge and skills held within the organization. The maintenance of this will indicate training needs. It is also possible to predict some of the skills which will be required in the future and which are not, at present, available.
- Organizational climate indices like turnover, absenteeism, short-term sickness, attitude surveys, grievances and strikes will sometimes indicate training needs as well as altering some aspects of the work situation.
- Efficiency indices like costs of labour and materials, quality of product, equipment utilization, cost of distribution, waste, machine down-time, late deliveries, repairs or customer complaints may indicate a shortfall in performance which can be improved by training.
- Requests by line management or surveys of their opinions are often used to build up the training plan.
- There is also often a training implication when new systems or new types of equipment are introduced.

Aspects of organizational effectiveness

The linking of training to the organizational context in which the work is done is fundamental to this level of analysis. One way of doing this, which I have found useful, is to talk regularly to managers about how they conceptualize 'effectiveness'. The method is based on critical incident analysis and the procedure is as follows:

- Target a function within the organization and arrange interviews with a representative sample of line managers and supervisors. Arrange to see the more senior ones first.
- Discuss aspects of organizational effectiveness with each member of your sample. Ask each to describe one or two incidents when things were going particularly well or badly; how the incident developed, what criteria were being used to judge 'well' or 'badly', what was the result of the incident in organizational terms.
- Use something like Figure 5.1 to classify the types of organizational effectiveness being used (and perhaps also offer the managers this list to prompt them). This framework for conceptualizing organizational effectiveness is derived from the work of Cameron (1980) and it is discussed much more fully in a later section when we examine how to assess changes in effectiveness as a result of training.
- As a result of this discussion try to understand the key results and priorities for the particular manager or supervisor. Discuss to what extent the present training provision helps with these key areas of effectiveness and also discuss whether some other form of training activity might help.
- An integration of the ideas generated in these interviews should give a clear view of what training and development might be able to do

---

Achieving goals of
   product or service quality
   output
   productivity
Increasing resourcefulness by
   increasing share of the market
   increasing employee versatility
   moving into new markets
Satisfying customers by
   improving organizational (or functional image)
   reducing complaints/returned material
   increasing proportion of on-time deliveries
Improving internal processes by
   increasing group cohesiveness
   improving quality of supervision
   helping to resolve departmental boundary problems
   increasing managers' ability to set realistic and tangible objectives for their departments

---

Figure 5.1　*Aspects of organizational effectiveness*

to improve the effectiveness of the particular function. This should be fed back to the senior managers in the function and the objectives for the training agreed. There will also be a need to secure the commitment of the senior managers to supporting the increased supervision or coaching and/or changing some of the work practices which are associated with low effectiveness.

Another way of linking training to the organizational requirement is to use a system of defining organizational effectiveness like the European model for Total Quality Management (EFQM, 1993), which describes nine areas considered to be those crucial to the success of any organization. The nine areas are listed below:

1 *Leadership*. How the executive team and all other managers inspire and drive total quality as the company's fundamental process for continuous improvement.
2 *Policy and strategy*. How the company incorporates the concept of total quality in the determination, communication, implementation, review and improvement of its policy and strategy.
3 *People management*. How the company releases the full potential of its people to improve its business continuously.
4 *Resources*. How the company improves its business continuously by optimization of financial, information and material resources.
5 *Processes*. How key and support processes are identified, reviewed and, if necessary, revised to ensure continuous improvement of the company's business.
6 *Customer satisfaction*. What the perception of external customers (direct and indirect) is of the company and of its products and services.
7 *People satisfaction*. How the company satisfies the needs and expectations of its people.
8 *Impact on society*. What the perception of the company is among the community at large.
9 *Business results*. What the company is achieving in relation to its planned business performance.

Regular and systematic review of the organization's activities in each of these nine areas will reveal aspects where improvements are necessary. Targets will be set for the next period (say, one year), and often training will be needed to help with the achievement of these targets.

Job data analysis

At the job data level of analysis it is necessary to discover what tasks need to be performed in order to do the job, how they should be performed and thus what needs to be learned in order to perform them well. McGehee and Thayer offer a number of techniques for carrying out such an analysis.

- Job descriptions will give an outline of the job and list typical duties and responsibilities. For some jobs these will change each year in response to setting new priorities.

- Job specifications are more detailed than job descriptions and should give a complete list of tasks. They may also include standards for judging satisfactory performance in the important tasks.
- Performance standards are usually phrased as objectives for the job and the targets or standards by which these will be judged.
- Actually doing the job oneself is a very effective method of analysis for specific tasks, but has obvious limitations in jobs where there are long gaps between performance and outcomes.
- Job observation or work sampling might also be used to look in detail at particular parts of the job.

Asking the job holder and the supervisor about the job is also a method suggested by McGehee and Thayer. This has been developed by the armed forces into a complex analysis by sending questionnaires to all incumbents and their supervisors, asking about frequency, importance and difficulty of various tasks which might be part of the job. The answers are analysed, usually by a computer programme called CODAP (Comprehensive Data Analysis Programme) which clusters the tasks, and this gives a complete specification of the job or, more usually, of a group of related jobs forming a trade structure. Training programmes are then designed based on decision trees like that in Figure 5.2.

When training programmes already exist, it is possible to estimate the relevance of the various topics covered to successful job performance. Ford and Wroten (1984) describe a method and its application for evaluating a training programme for police patrol officers. Subject matter experts (i.e. patrol officers, sergeants and police officers from other cities) independently rated the importance of knowledge, skills and attitudes (KSA) learned in training for successful job performance. The extent to which each area of KSA was necessary for satisfactory performance was then calculated as a 'content validity ratio'. The training curriculum was then examined and the amount of time devoted to each topic linked to the content validity. Of 237 KSAs rated as important for job performance, 57 were not included in the training programme. Some were thought to be trainable as well as important for job success, and were included in later programmes.

Goldstein (1992) has suggested an alternative method of correlating job analysis information with the amount of time devoted to topics during training. Using this method, Newman (1985) assessed a two-week programme for cook foremen. Newman had 85 subject matter experts rate the proposed KSAs in terms of their importance to the job, difficulty of learning and where best learned. As an indicator of content validity Newman correlated the job importance ratings with training emphasis (i.e. time spent). For cooking and baking KSAs the correlation was 0.52; for KSAs involved with supervision and administration the

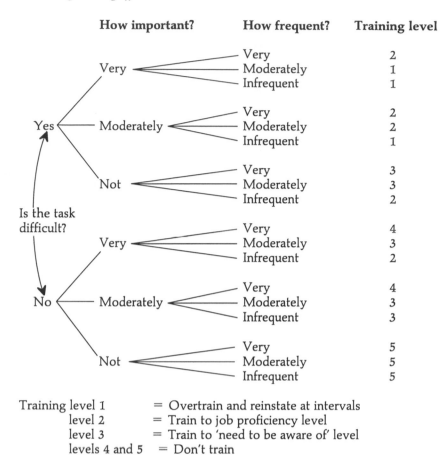

How important?	How frequent?	Training level
Very	Very	2
	Moderately	1
	Infrequent	1
Moderately	Very	2
	Moderately	2
	Infrequent	1
Not	Very	3
	Moderately	3
	Infrequent	2
Very	Very	4
	Moderately	3
	Infrequent	2
Moderately	Very	4
	Moderately	3
	Infrequent	3
Not	Very	5
	Moderately	5
	Infrequent	5

Training level 1 = Overtrain and reinstate at intervals
level 2 = Train to job proficiency level
level 3 = Train to 'need to be aware of' level
levels 4 and 5 = Don't train

Figure 5.2 *The difficulty/frequency/importance matrix*

correlation was 0.55. This research may eventually produce benchmarks for deciding at what level of correlation the content validity can be said to be satisfactory. It has already produced a system for revealing any serious mismatch between content and job requirements.

Faley and Sandstrom (1985) describe a method of assessing the relevance of the content of a training programme by using the Position Analysis Questionnaire (PAQ). This is a structured job analysis questionnaire containing 194 job elements. The elements are grouped under six headings as follows:

1 *Information input.* Where and how does the worker obtain the information used in the job?
2 *Mental processes.* What reasoning, decision making, planning, etc. is involved in the job?
3 *Work output.* What physical activities does the worker perform and what tools, etc. are used?

4 *Relationships*. What relationships with other people are required in the job?
5 *Job context*. In what social or physical contexts is the work performed?
6 *Other job characteristics*. What activities and conditions other than those already described affect the worker?

Training programme analysts used the PAQ to analyse the programme as if it was a job. Job incumbents also used the PAQ to analyse the job itself. The profile comparison identified aspects that were over- or underemphasized.

All three methods have the strength of firmly defining the training requirement in terms of job performance. It sounds rather obvious but it may be necessary. In my experience, trainers have a tendency to concentrate on what they enjoy teaching (or what they believe the trainees will enjoy learning) and the training content can drift away from the job requirement. In one particular programme which we evaluated, half of the theoretical content was not relevant to successful job performance.

Person analysis

At the individual level of analysis the intention is to assess performance levels against those required in the job. Theoretically, a training programme can then be designed for each individual to close the gap between present and desired levels of performance. McGehee and Thayer offer a long list of techniques by which individual training needs can be identified. These include the following:

- Performance appraisal, which identifies weaknesses and areas for improvement as well as strengths
- Observation and work sampling, or testing of knowledge and skills required in the job
- Interviews and questionnaires
- Devising situations like role-plays, case studies, business games and in-baskets. Recently, these have often been combined in assessment centres where identifying development needs rather than selection is the main purpose.

A word of caution needs to be introduced here. I am using the word 'need' to mean an observable discrepancy in performance produced by lack of skill, and not to mean a job holder's expression of preference for, or interest in, a particular programme. It is also worth noting that a performance deficiency does not necessarily imply a training need. For instance, Mager and Pipe (1970) recommend the algorithm in Figure 5.3. This should remind us that job situation factors like organizational culture, structure and reward systems may be more powerful controllers of job behaviour than the abilities of the individuals in the job.

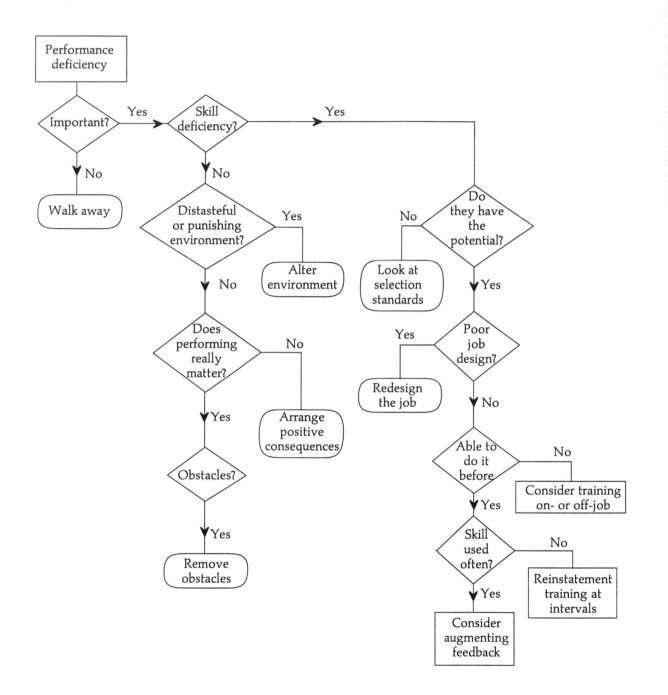

Figure 5.3 *Analysing performance problems*
(Adapted from Mager and Pipe, 1970)

> **Rowland, in 1970, reported on a survey of 4000 managers in which he asked, 'Why do subordinates fail?' The most popular answers given, listed in order of frequency, are shown below:**
>
> **They do not know what they are supposed to do**
> **They do not know how to do it**
> **They do not know why they should do it**
> **There are obstacles beyond their control**
> **They do not think it will work**
> **They think that their way is better**
> **They were not motivated (or poor attitude)**
> **They were incapable of doing it (or poor skills)**
> **There was insufficient time to do it**
> **They were working on the wrong priority items**
> **They thought that they were doing it**
> **Poor management**
> **Personal problems**

An interesting development in person analysis for managerial jobs has been the recent emphasis on observable behaviour rather than abstract qualities. This usually takes the form of defining the 'competencies' which are important for successful performance in a particular job and appraising the incumbent against these competencies. (Competencies include: developing people, analysing problems, representing part of the organization, chairing meetings, resolving disputes, developing new procedures, making decisions, etc. Many lists are available and the key results areas of most jobs can be defined in less than a dozen competencies.) Where the appraisal is done as a joint exercise between a manager and his or her supervisor it often results in a statement of development needs to be met by on-the-job tasking, etc., perhaps combined with off-the-job learning opportunities. It is also becoming increasingly common for assessment centres to be used in this way, i.e. to focus on key competence areas. This can then be used to identify individual development needs within the context of what that particular part of the organization identifies as key results areas.

Integration of the three levels of analysis

Training needs analyses often concentrate on the person analysis level and neglect the links with organizational goals which are necessary to ensure that the training is effective in advancing the cause of the company.

An early attempt to avoid this was the use of the 'systems approach' to training. This was based upon detailed job analysis and the writing of behavioural objectives. The process followed the sequence shown in Figure 5.4.

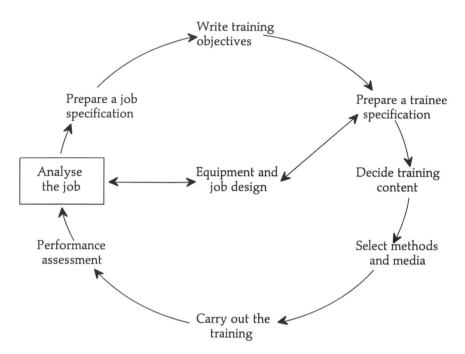

Figure 5.4 *A systematic training cycle*

This method of designing training to meet individual, job and organizational needs has been used by the armed forces for many years and it has proved to be very successful in the development of technical staff. The approach is comprehensive, but rather cumbersome, as the job analysis needs to be repeated every other year to cope with changes in responsibilities, equipment and techniques. It has, however, great strengths where the jobs which are necessary for organizational effectiveness can be clearly defined in terms of tasks and standards.

Where jobs are less easy to define, or where they vary because of considerable innovation by incumbents, an alternative method for integrating training needs is to start from the business plan and cascade objectives down through the organization. An example of good practice was given by a petrochemicals company with which we were involved as consultants. First, the chief executive decided his objectives for the coming year and held a half-day meeting with his general managers to explain his objectives and then to allow each of them to develop his or her own objectives and share them with the other general managers. This formed the basis of the business plan. Next, each general manager cascaded objectives down through his or her part of the company by organizing between four and six half-day sessions in sequence so that the higher order objectives were broken down and interpreted. At each level some negotiation of the objectives was necessary in order to incorporate the realities at that level. The result of this process was that each of the departments, and, indeed, the individual managers, had negotiated what their objectives were for the next year and knew how these integrated vertically right up to those of the chief executive. (The sequence of top-down was important. In one part of the company it got out of phase, and it was noticeable that here the objectives were not integrated and there was not the same sense of purpose.)

The next phase was to incorporate these objectives into the annual performance appraisal by each manager agreeing with his or her supervisor the targets which represented the key results' areas. Each key result area was analysed (by discussion between manager and supervisor) for the competencies required to achieve it, and then the training needs were identified in terms of competencies thought desirable but not well developed. The training department was thus able to collect lists of competencies to be developed and, by clustering these, produce a training plan.

The database derived from this cascade process has produced information for job descriptions, recruitment and bonus payments. It has also produced a profile of the managers in the company in terms of skills available (defined as competencies). This was examined and discussed at board level in order to establish longer-term development activities required for the management group to meet future challenges. The process has proved to be very powerful in motivating the managers—they can see exactly how their contribution fits into the overall effort and they are convinced that the company cares about their development.

A third method of integrating the three levels of need is the use of a Total Quality Management analysis of the various parts of the organization. For instance, with the European model (EFQM, 1993) outlined above, the process is intended to produce continuous development in each of the nine elements. A small multi-disciplinary team discusses each of the nine elements with line managers in a part of the organization. The team is usually invited and asked to help rather than the process being considered as an inspection. As a result of these discussions, areas for improvement are identified and agreed, then targets are set for improved performance. A date (say, one year on) is also set when progress towards these targets will be reviewed. In order to achieve some of these targets, training will be required for managers and supervisors and, perhaps, for other employees. The identification of training needs is at an individual level—what each needs in order to assist with meeting targets—but the process is integrated with the organizational requirement for improved effectiveness in that part of the organization.

Perhaps this is a good place to pause and think about how the training needs are identified in your organization.

- What methods are being used to identify needs at the organizational level?
- What methods at the job level?
- What methods at the person level?
- How well are the three levels integrated? Which predominates and why?
- How well is training linked to the business plan? What could be done to strengthen this link? Who could do it? What can you do?

Latham (1988) states that, 'Organizational support for training should be operationally defined as the extent to which training objectives are linked to organizational objectives, the extent to which the training objectives change as soon as there is a change in the organization's strategic emphasis, and the extent to which training progress is viewed together with the progress made in achieving the business plan.'

What is the extent of the support for training in your organization?

Summary

The identification of training needs is a complex area, and requires more detailed analysis than is possible in a book about evaluation. The emphasis placed upon it here reflects my view that the manner in which needs are identified is an important factor in the design of the evaluation. For instance, if the identification of training needs is synonymous with asking people which courses they would like to attend, then the only *valid* form of evaluation will be to assess the extent to which the courses were provided. The retrospective question, of whether attendance on these courses has brought any benefit for the organizational funds invested, may be posed, but it cannot be answered, because the criteria against which changes in job performance and effectiveness are to be assessed have not been defined as part of the needs analysis.

6 Sequencing learning experiences

Training in its organizational context

Having decided that a need can be met by some form of training, and having defined the changes in performance against which the training will be evaluated, the next area which needs attention is the sequencing of the learning. The word 'learning' is chosen deliberately to emphasize that delivering training is not the same thing as actually learning something when taking part in the activity. The first model of training which we looked at (Figure 4.1) is essentially an input model, as the changes in performance are expected rather than built into the process. To put this model into its organizational context gives us something like Figure 6.1 (which is adapted from Berger, 1977).

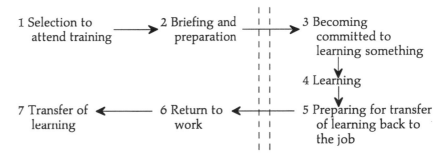

(The vertical lines between stages 2 and 3, and between 5 and 6, are intended to represent the distance between the job situation and the training activity)

Figure 6.1 *Training in its organizational context*

Pre-activity learner support

Selection

We have discussed above, at some length, the selection of the right people for a particular training activity. Here are some questions which

I would ask you to consider in relation to the quality of the selection process in your own organization:

1 Do you question the participants at the beginning of a training event about why they have come?
2 What proportion attend because someone else had been booked for the training, but couldn't come?
3 How many attend because it is their turn to do some training this year?
4 What proportion have asked for this programme because they know of someone else who enjoyed it?
5 How many of them know what kind of person is most likely to benefit from the particular learning which is being offered?
6 How many of the trainees are tested before the programme to ensure that they are ready for training?
7 How often do you send someone back because the training is not appropriate for them?
8 For what proportion of the participants is the training 'just in time'?

The training can be efficient in doing what it sets out to do, but it cannot be effective if the wrong people are attending.

Briefing and preparation

The second phase of the model (Figure 6.1) implies that, before the training takes place, the developmental objectives should be established between the person who is to learn something and the person who is nominating him or her. Most adult learning is motivated by attempts to reach goals. Locke and Latham (1990), on the basis of extensive research, specify the relationship between goals and performance as follows:

1 Individuals who have specific and challenging goals perform better than those who have easy goals.
2 Specific goals are much more effective than general goals like 'do your best' or 'learn what you can'.
3 Feedback on how well the goal is being achieved is necessary.
4 Individuals must accept the goals set.

In order to tap this source of motivation, it is clear that the participants must fully understand the objectives for the programme and, to some extent, accept them as their personal objectives.

What form does the pre-programme briefing take in your organization?

● Who does the briefing?
● Are learning objectives clarified and agreed?
● Do the supervisors/managers understand them?
● Was any pre-programme activity required? Was it carried out?

The vertical lines between phases 2 and 3 in Figure 6.1 represent the distance between the job and the training. If nothing happens at phase 2, then at phase 3, in the training event, the first day is spent in trying to commit people to the learning objectives. If the training is on-job, this is not too serious, but if it is off-job, there is a danger that the objectives set will be personal development or therapy objectives which have little to do with improving performance in the job. Have you looked at the flipcharts which adorn the walls of many an interpersonal skills programme and which state, 'My objectives for the week are . . .'? Do they reflect learning which will improve job performance?

The sequence of the programme

The learning situations themselves should be sequenced so that people can use various styles of learning and integrate them into a meaningful whole. A useful model to consider is that of Kolb (1984) which is based on adults learning from their experience. Figure 6.2 illustrates the cycle of learning.

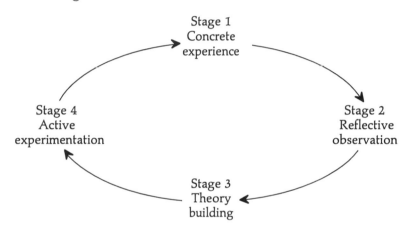

Figure 6.2   *The Kolb cycle of learning*

The theory requires activity in all four stages for effective learning. This implies that there should be some concrete experience, with the learners involving themselves fully and openly, and some reflective observation, where the learners are helped to step back and reflect on the experience. These two stages should be followed by a phase when they are helped to integrate their observations into a logically sound framework, i.e. they alter their general theory of 'how things like this work'. The final stage is to encourage active experimentation so that they can test their theories and use them as bases for decision making and problem solving.

Few people are equally strong in all these phases, and the learning situation should offer more support in the stages in which they are weakest. It is not too difficult to set up experiences and to assist the learners to analyse what they have experienced, but encouraging them to incorporate the analysis into *their* way of thinking takes a great deal of time, effort and ingenuity. Testing their learning in other, similar situations takes time, more time than is usually available in training events, and this phase is usually left to chance in the hope that they will try it at work.

A better process would be to *ensure* that they can try out the ideas in the work situation by involving colleagues and supervisors in the development process—in other words, to incorporate some of the aspects of action learning. During the learning, some emphasis should be placed on examining what is being learned for utility back on-the-job, and plans should be made for transferring the learning. Usually this will involve an action plan which anticipates some of the organizational constraints on introducing change and identifies likely sources of support, perhaps by using some form of force-field analysis.

If all the first five phases in Figure 6.1 have been done properly, then it should be possible to return to work and transfer the learning. Often, however, the learning 'burns off' on re-entry because no-one in the workplace carries out a debriefing and offers support. The most common experience is to be greeted by, 'Had a good time? We have been busy while you have been away, but we have kept some of it for you and it's all in your in-tray.' On emerging from the in-tray two weeks later, the training programme seems to be a historical event.

One area of training, that of interpersonal skills, has a particularly poor record in transferring, and it is worth looking at the model in order to isolate why this should be so. It is a confused area because many trainers are actually trying to change *attitudes* but are calling it *'skills training'*. Underlying this is a belief that if people's attitudes are changed this will lead to behaviour changes, i.e. improved interpersonal skills. There is very little published evidence to support this belief.

On the other hand, psychomotor skills training does transfer well, and it is probably because it has the following characteristics. It is possible to:

- isolate critical skills from job samples and specify what they look like in some detail
- demonstrate the skill, break it down into phases and practise it, giving feedback throughout the practice to narrow the gap between actual and desired performance
- transfer the skill to the workplace and give further feedback until the level achieved in training reaches the operational standard.

In order for the training to be successful the following conditions need to be met:

- The analysis of the critical skills is done with great precision, often including detailed task analysis.
- The feedback in training is very similar to that of the job situation, i.e. high environmental fidelity is essential.

- The amount of transfer is directly proportional to the number of elements common to both training and job situations.

The model usually used in interpersonal skills training ignores important aspects of this skills model:

- Very generalized sets of behaviours are called skills (e.g. 'communication').
- The feedback given is artificial and nothing like that available in the work situation (i.e. no environmental fidelity).
- The learning activity takes place off-the-job and there are very few elements common to both the training and the job. (One of the crucial elements, for instance, is the actual people one has to work with.)

One successful method of training people in interpersonal skills was developed by Goldstein and Sorcher (1974). They adopted the principles of social learning theory and applied them to a programme for training supervisors in behaviours like:

1 Orientating a new employee
2 Giving training on-the-job
3 Motivating the poor performer
4 Handling discrimination complaints
5 Conducting a performance review.

The training sessions were of two-hour duration off-job and were structured as follows:

1 The importance of the topic to the success of the job was emphasized by the trainers and agreed by the supervisors.
2 A video was shown which portrayed a model effectively handling the type of situation to be examined.
3 Key points were drawn from the modelling.
4 Group discussion took place on the effectiveness and relevance of the modelled behaviours.
5 Role-playing by the supervisors with feedback from the group.

The supervisors then went back to the job and reported in the next session (two weeks later) whether they had encountered the situation and how they had responded to it. This method of training has great theoretical strength in that it incorporates all of the phases of the Kolb cycle. Actual situations are demonstrated, discussed and role-played. Reflection on the key points is required and active testing in the actual work situation is followed by further reflection and discussion.

The training reported by Goldstein and Sorcher was evaluated in terms of productivity levels in the work areas for which the four supervisors were responsible. These showed an improvement in three out of the four areas and a decrease in the fourth area. There were decreases in productivity in the areas of responsibility of all of the four supervisors who had been selected as 'controls' and not trained.

The book by Goldstein and Sorcher is an excellent text, unique in the training literature in that it starts from a thoroughly researched theory, adapts it to a field situation and tests it. It has led to a number of studies further investigating behavioural role modelling as a training technique. The best of these to date has been produced by Latham and Saari (1979). Faced with the problem of training 100 supervisors in an organization, they decided to follow the same training procedure as Goldstein and Sorcher (indeed, they used the models recorded on video by Sorcher). The foremen could not all be trained at once, so groups were selected for early training and those to be trained later were used (unknowingly) as controls.

The design of the study was:

Test 1	Train	Test 2	Train	Test 3	
Gp A	A	A	–	A	n = 20
Gp B	–	B	B	B	n = 20
Similar baseline		Expect A better		Expect similar	

The testing was done at three levels, those of 'learning', 'behaviour' and 'results'. *Learning* was assessed by a test of knowledge of the key aspects of the behaviour thought likely to be successful in the critical incidents trained. *Behaviour* was assessed by observation and reports from managers, and *results* from measures of productivity in the sections for which the supervisors were responsible. The training group was better than the controls at all three levels.

Behaviour modelling has become popular as a method of management and supervisor training. Mayer and Russell (1987) were able to review 14 studies conducted in field settings. The research revealed that trainees *react* positively to behaviour modelling training and also that it is effective at the *learning* level. The evidence concerning the effectiveness of it in influencing *performance* is more equivocal.

Explanations put forward to account for this variable transfer of learning back to the job usually include descriptions of unreceptive work cultures. This may, however, be too simple. The theoretical basis for transfer of social learning is derived from the work of Bandura (1977, 1986). Bandura would argue that cognitive mediating variables play a part in transfer and that the most important of these is 'self-efficacy'. This is defined as a self-judgement of how able one is to successfully carry through a course of action required to deal with a particular situation. The level of this will depend upon perceived mastery of knowledge and skills, but also on the perception of the work situation. The implication here is that there should be some support available in the work situation to enhance self-efficacy for those in whom it is relatively low. Those in whom it is relatively high will be able to use the skills learned without this support. According to Bandura (1986), the level of self-efficacy can be raised by:

- enactive mastery by actually performing the task successfully
- vicarious experience by seeing someone else similar to yourself performing the task successfully.

This returns us to the point made earlier, that high environmental fidelity is needed in order to achieve high levels of transfer in skills training, but it goes further in encouraging us to think of the developing manager as increasing in self-efficacy—in other words, increasing knowledge and skills and also the perception of being confident in using them.

A quite different theoretical approach is described in the excellent book on interpersonal skills training by Rackham and Morgan (1977), who treated the learning process as information processing (stage-by-stage reduction of uncertainty by use of feedback). The categories of behaviour to be learned were selected on the basis of their having a critical bearing on the effectiveness of job behaviour. For instance, with appraisal interviewing:

High levels of:	Low levels of:
seeking information	proposing
testing understanding	disagreeing
summarizing	blocking
building	difficulty stating

The training was intended first to provide a vocabulary to allow the participants to identify categories of behaviour, and secondly to give feedback to reduce the discrepancy between the actual use of the categories and participants' perception of how frequently they used them. The feedback was given on samples of behaviour at work, recorded by an observer. The key aspect of all this is the integration between tracking of behaviour change and training. There is a continual cycle of evaluation, feedback and training, leading to further evaluation, feedback and training. This is a true skills model, and Rackham and Morgan describe a number of successful applications of behaviour analysis in training. Their book represents a very impressive body of work.

Patrick, Michael and Moore (1986) describe six types of learning: learning facts, discriminations, concepts, rules, procedures and problem solving. The categories are largely based on Gagne's work (1970) and reflect behavioural research on learning. The course design proceeds from:

- identifying the types of learning required
- selecting a suitable method for each type

- sequencing the programme from the lowest to the highest type of learning required.

Each of these three approaches (behaviour modelling described by Goldstein and Sorcher, behaviour analysis used by Rackham and Morgan and designing learning in the way suggested by Patrick, Michael and Moore) has the strength of being founded on a sound theoretical base which gives some unity and purpose to the design of the programme, rather than the *ad hoc* pragmatism which is more typical of trainers. Some unity to the design will increase the likelihood of learning and also its transfer to the job. Programmes which are made up of a collection of learning situations, each used because it has proved interesting in the past, usually do not have a unifying design and the learning does not develop in a way which aids transfer.

It is possible, and often useful, to examine the delivery phase of the programme in some detail. As well as the overall course structure which we have been discussing, it is also worth examining the use of objectives, the methods and media and the use of feedback. Questions which might be posed are listed in Figure 6.3.

Figure 6.3 lists more questions on the use of evaluative feedback during the programme than on any other area. This reflects my view that learning is a cyclical process and, therefore, that feedback is necessary at each stage in order to evaluate how present performance differs from that desired. This feedback should be given before new learning takes place. An end-of-course discussion is usually too late to allow for this.

Transfer of learning

As we can see in Figure 6.1, the final phase in the training cycle is the incorporation of the new ways of thinking or doing things into normal work. Often this is left to the individual, and the (unstated) implication is that the individual has the motivation and the ability to introduce such changes.

We are back in the area of self-efficacy here. People who judge themselves low have difficulty in coping with environmental demands. They imagine that potential difficulties are more formidable than is actually the case and they dwell on their personal deficiencies. People who are strong in self-efficacy focus on the demands of the situation and treat obstacles as a challenge. Self-efficacy has been found to increase when experience fails to support fears and when the skills learned help to master the situation which was felt to be threatening. Much of this is to do with ability to predict and manage perceived threats. How can we increase self-efficacy in a training programme?

- Maximize the similarity between the training situation and the job, if necessary by carrying out the training in phases with job experience interspersed.

Objectives

- Have the tutorial staff access to a copy of the current objectives?
- Are the objectives clear and unambiguous?
- Can the objectives be completely met by this training event or is some continuation by on-the-job training required?
- To what extent are the tutors familiar with the trainees' learning objectives? How are they taking these into account?

Course structure

- On what principles is the course structured?
- Is there a satisfactory balance between practice, reflection and theoretical input?
- How satisfactory is the duration of the course and the length of the working day?
- Does the balance of the course reflect the different degrees of importance attached to the objectives?

Methods and media

- On what basis have the methods been chosen?
- Are behavioural methods being used where behaviour change is expected?
- Are cognitive schema being built up where problem-solving is expected?
- Are optimal methods being used, given the characteristics of the learners?
- Do methods and media provide variety and encourage learning?
- What is the quality and readability of handouts, computer-based training material and training aids?

Evaluative feedback

- What form of assessment of progress is being used during the programme?
- Is each assessment method reliable and timely?
- How is feedback given to the trainees?
- How is feedback used by the tutors? Is there enough flexibility to allow for individual remedial work, etc.?
- Are summarizing and consolidating sessions built into the programme?
- Are evaluative reports written on courses? To whom are they sent? Is any action taken as a result of these reports?

Figure 6.3 *Questions about a programme*

- Provide a wide range of experience of what is being learned so that the principles can be applied to situations which do not exactly fit the procedure. If we divide the material to be learned into three levels, this implies spending some time on the 'analysis' level:

    3 Analysis of situations to decide which procedures are likely to be successful

    ↑

    2 Learning procedures or ways of doing things

    ↑

    1 Learning isolated pieces of information

- Ensure that what is being learned in training will be supported and rewarded in the workplace. There is clearly a role for the supervisor or manager here; he or she must be a party to the training and transfer.
- Goal setting is important because without it people will have a poor basis for judging how they are progressing. Clear measures of progress are essential for increasing self-efficacy. Trainees should be deterred from setting very difficult goals as those who give up are often those who self-impose very high standards and then feel no sense of accomplishment because they fail to reach them.

Increasing self-efficacy is only one aspect of maximizing transfer from training to work situations. The literature on transfer offers some help to those concerned by suggesting other important aspects.

1 For *initiation* of transfer (the willingness to try to apply the new learning) the emphasis should be on:
   - goal setting and action plans (Baldwin and Ford, 1988)
   - pre-course briefing and post-course support (Baldwin and Ford, 1988)
   - management support for training (Goldstein, 1993)
   - over-learning of material (Goldstein, 1993)
   - higher self-efficacy (Mathieu *et al*, 1993).
2 For *maintenance* of transfer (after it has been initiated):
   - reinstatement training/relearning at intervals (Adams, 1987)
   - relapse prevention (Marx, 1982)
   - extrinsic reward of some sort (Goldstein, 1993)
   - high self-efficacy to persist despite disappointment (Bandura, 1986).
3 For *near* transfer (where the job situation is accurately specified and can be simulated in training), the emphasis should be on:
   - maximizing the identical elements between the training and the job (Adams, 1987)
   - high psychological fidelity (so that the trainees perceive the training situation to be very like the job) (Goldstein, 1993)
   - over-learning the procedures (Goldstein, 1993).
4 For *far* transfer (where the requirement is for applying the learning to a variety of situations):
   - teaching general principles (McGehee and Thayer, 1961)
   - learning in a variety of relevant situations (Baldwin and Ford, 1988)
   - application of the learning to new situations both during the training and afterwards, with encouragement from the trainers and others (Goldstein, 1993).

It should be noted that trying to maximize *near* transfer is likely to hinder *far* transfer, as a rather stereotyped set of behaviours will be learned and these may not be suitable for varying situations. The implication is that, before the training is designed, it is necessary to specify the type of transfer intended.

One other finding from the literature on transfer of training is worth noting here. Retention is especially difficult when there is a significant time delay between the learning and its application on the job. This is not so serious where perceptual/motor skills are involved, but it is serious where the skills are primarily based on cognitive/knowledge processes. Wetzel, Konoske and Montague (1983) have shown that these skills, based upon knowledge of procedures, can be subject to rapid and extensive loss in a few weeks. Another instance of this was described by Prophet (1976), who showed that psychomotor flight skills are retained for many months longer than procedural flight skills. Hagman and Rose (1983) reviewed the retention of on-job skills such as emergency procedures which were infrequently practised, and found that they often showed deterioration to the point of being problematic. It is common knowledge that emergency and safety procedures need reinstatement training at intervals. What the literature is telling us is that this is also true of topics covered in other programmes. If the new ideas have not been applied fairly soon (probably within three months) after the learning experience there is a risk that they will be lost. This seems to me to raise important questions about generic programmes like those which are designed for all who reach a certain level in management. It also underlines the value of approaches like 'just-in-time' training.

This might be a good place to pause for thought. The problems raised by transfer of training have encouraged many organizations to take training nearer to the workplace. We have already mentioned behaviour modelling and behaviour analysis where training in interpersonal skills and their application at work are integrated. There is also the whole field of action learning (see, for example, Pedler, 1983) where the transfer problem is avoided by using actual work problems as media for training. What is it like in *your* organization? How do you attempt to maximize transfer? Do you have any post-programme learner support?

1 **What form does the post-programme briefing take?**
2 **Who does it?**
3 **Are action plans reviewed and priorities set?**
4 **What constraints are being put on the trainees' ability to apply the learning?**
5 **What support is available to close the gap between levels of achievement on the programme and competent job performance?**
6 **What changes are being achieved in terms of:**
 ● **different individual performance levels?**
 ● **increased levels of organizational effectiveness?**
7 **What criteria for effectiveness of training are being used?**

7 Training in its organizational context

An evaluation of the training process will often include some examination of the organizational context in which the training need is identified and in which the learning is to be applied. I have suggested, by the definition adopted in the Introduction, that the training function should be contributing to the organizational goals by increasing the effectiveness of the work being carried out in particular parts of the organization. This contribution can be seen to have two main aspects: maintaining the present skills pool; and preparing employees for new challenges.

Maintaining the skills pool

One important responsibility of trainers in most organizations is the provision of induction and initial training. A wide range of methods is available for this purpose and the evaluative questions are most likely to be about the suitability of the process used for the particular organization. For instance:

- What kinds of methods are being used and how well do these suit the people coming in?
- How well does the content match the requirement of the trainees? What assumptions are being made about initial capabilities?
- What assumptions are being made about closing the gap between end-of-training ability and job proficiency?
- How flexible is the control system to allow for peaks and troughs of the recruiting process?
- How good are the managers at providing on-the-job training?
- How good is the integration of the induction training with continuing development of skills on-the-job?

A second aspect of looking at the maintenance of the skills pool involves looking at the various methods of delivery which are being used by the organization. To assist in this, the following questions might be useful:

- Which programmes are being run internally and which are being contracted out? On what grounds were the decisions made to run them in this way?
- What is the range of methods of delivery in use? Distance learning? Paper-based texts? Video packages? On-job? Team development? Learner-centred discovery? etc.
- To what extent are these various methods appropriate for the topic and for the type of trainee?
- To what extent is the training provision encouraging people to continue learning within the job and thus become more adaptable to changing circumstances (as opposed to emphasizing routines and procedures which must be followed)?
- What investigations are being carried out into the use of new methods and technology?
- What aspects of learning effectiveness are being considered? Is user acceptability being examined?
- Is anyone carrying out cost-effectiveness comparisons? Is it likely that some of the training could be left to on-job development?
- What retraining is being given to maintain standards on little-used procedures or skills? What is the cost of not providing this training?
- To what extent is training devolved into departments? How active are line managers in the training of their people?

Preparing for new challenges

The questions about how well the training function is contributing to the maintenance of the skills pool essentially cover 'What are you doing and how well are you doing it?' When thinking about new challenges for the organization, the question becomes the more difficult 'What should you be doing to prepare for the future?'

In an ideal organizational context, the training function should be drawing up plans for the development of management and workforce to enable the organization to change in desired directions. The development of human resources within the organization will include selection, assessment of performance, estimation of potential and some form of career planning for individuals as well as the overall manpower planning for the future. It is clear that training should contribute to this process and should be integrated into the planning of it. Much of the contribution of training will be the maintenance of the skills pool which we have already discussed. Some, however, will be estimating the shortfall in capability for likely future trends or legislation. There is also the challenge of predicting new areas of opportunity and the KSAs necessary to secure these.

If the training manager is to make a contribution to the future development of the organization, he or she should be informed and consulted at an early stage in the planning of organizational change. If training is to be fully integrated into organizational development, the role of the trainers and their managers becomes much more wide-ranging. Essentially they become internal consultants, as well as maintaining the more traditional role. Not all training managers are willing to take on this role for, as we shall see, the skills involved are very different from those traditionally associated with training.

Training has developed from a tradition of activities which helped individuals to perform identified tasks within jobs. Changing the focus from clearly specified jobs to the future well-being of the organization implies a profound change in the skills required of the trainers. The skills of job analysis and in-class presentation of material, which are widely present in the population of trainers, become much less valuable than the problem-solving and political skills required for working successfully with line managers. These latter skills are not widely distributed among trainers. There is also the crucial question of the capacity of the training manager to make changes. He or she usually reports to the personnel manager and thus is often not in a sufficiently powerful position to be proactive in planning changes within the organization.

Perhaps it is worth while contrasting the traditional role of training departments with what they would be required to do if they were to function in the way being suggested.

- The traditional role involves training needs analysis at the job and individual levels, then the development and running of courses. It is largely a role of responding to requests and it is a fairly stable function which is well understood by management.
- The proactive role involves individual and group counselling. It is largely a role of catalyst and coordinator of management workshops and problem-solving groups. Its primary focus is on developing human resources policy, particularly where this involves changing the culture. The role is complex and may not be well understood by management.

The implications of this second type of role are that the training manager must be more involved with policy making and thus needs greater access to information. In order to carry out such a role successfully, the training manager and the trainers who will be working in functions need to develop their boundary management by:

- acquiring the resources to provide services
- building relationships and promoting their image
- protecting their integrity and position
- coordinating activities with other roles and functions
- exercising influence over key decision makers.

There is also the issue of knowledge of other disciplines like recruiting, job evaluation and design, manpower planning and organizational development. If we turn back to the discussion about trying to change the interaction between the people and the job situation in which they found themselves (see Figure 4.2), it is clear that someone will need to be thinking about structures, cultures, job design, reward systems and selection. The training manager will often be unable to do this alone, and the implication is that a team of specialists will be needed to plan and carry through organizational changes.

The training policy document

The interrelationship between the training department and its organizational context is often encapsulated in the training policy. Examination of this document often raises questions, and amendment of it, by negotiation, can often improve the training department's contribution to the maintenance of skills and the preparation for future challenges.

A typical training policy document will include sections on the purpose of training, the networks connecting training to line managers and an outline of responsibilities for the various stages in the training process. An outline of what each section might contain is given below.

The *purpose of training* section might include:

- General statements about the relationship between training and organizational performance, perhaps how it assists in:
  - helping people who are new to jobs to become effective as soon as possible
  - the maintenance of necessary skills and abilities
  - improvements in standards
  - improvements in flexibility
  - preparation for new challenges to the organization
- A statement about the commitment to develop individuals so that they can realize their potential, innovate within their jobs, increase their satisfaction, etc.

The *networks* section might include:

- On which organizational committees training interests must be represented so that needs at the organizational level can be identified as early as possible
- When project groups or task forces should copy their minutes to the training manager for training implications to be identified
- Which organizational (and/or functional) committees are responsible for identifying future training needs, monitoring present provision and setting priorities
- What arrangements there are for linking the training department to the line managers (liaison officers, trainers with specific responsibilities, local training officers, etc.)
- The responsibility of line managers for identifying needs, establishing contact, integrating off-job training with on-job tasking and supervision and evaluating training effectiveness.

The *training process* section would normally be an outline of the process and allocation of responsibilities between line managers, personnel specialists, trainers and trainees:

- The setting of objectives in terms of improved performance of some part of the organization. Within this the trainers (or training manager) can set training objectives, but the setting and achievement of the overall objective is the responsibility of the head of function/department/whatever
- The options for achieving the objectives and what else must change to support any learning. Who is responsible for reviewing structure, climate, reward systems, etc?
- How decisions are to be made on whether training should be given on-job or off-job, using company trainers or contracting it out
- What must happen before the training? What are the responsibilities of the manager, the trainees and the trainers for the pre-programme briefing and setting of individual learning objectives?
- What expectations are there for the contribution of line managers to the training?
- Who is responsible for evaluating progress during training?
- What expectation is there for post-programme learner support:
  - the format for post-programme discussion of utility of learning
  - the reviewing of action plans and setting of priorities and review dates
- Who is responsible for evaluating changes in individual levels of performance and increases in aspects of organizational effectiveness?

The outline above is intended to suggest what an evaluator might look for in a training policy document. The format and the detail will, of course, depend upon the management style of the organization in question. Such a document, with clear statements as to the purpose of training and who is responsible for the various aspects of it, is likely to be necessary if the effectiveness of training is to be evaluated. It is unlikely that members of the training department will be able to do this on their own as they will not have access to the performance data necessary. It is also the case that, in many large organizations, the responsibility for training seems to have been allocated to the training manager. This cannot be right as the responsibility for training and developing employees lies with their manager, and time and effort spent on this should be regarded as an important part of the manager's job. The role of the trainers is to provide a service to management, to assist them with *their* responsibility for training. I have run workshops on evaluation of training in many training departments, and often the trainers have stated that line managers do not accept this responsibility. It is therefore my opinion that in many organizations it is worth while spelling out the responsibilities in a policy document which is negotiated with the senior management team.

Summary

I started this part of the book with a statement that it is often worth while to evaluate a training programme by examining the processes by which it was designed and delivered. My basic premise is that the purpose of training is to improve the performance of individuals and thus increase the effectiveness of the organization. It follows that our first concern must be with the link between the training activities offered and aspects of organizational effectiveness. The first questions which should be posed are therefore:

- What changes are expected to result from this programme in terms of individual performance levels?
- How are these changes linked to organizational effectiveness?
- How do these changes relate to overall corporate objectives?

Models of training that take into account the work context are examples of organizational change based upon learning activities. They are more appropriate than educational models when the intention is to change the way in which the work is done.

Accurate identification of training needs is difficult and takes a good deal of time. It is, however, crucial to the success of the training process. Needs can be identified at the organizational level by looking at the *strategic* plans for the future, the *tactical* plans for next year and the day-to-day *operational* problems. They can also be identified at the job and individual levels. If the training is to be effective, some attempt must be made to integrate the three levels and thus invest in training which will benefit the organization as well as develop individuals.

If any particular training activity is to be an effective learning process, three elements should be present:

1 The pre-programme preparation should be carried out to bring forward participants who are attending the right course for the right reasons.
2 The programme should be designed as a continuous set of activities structured to complement each other in facilitating learning.
3 Post-programme learning support is necessary to extend the training period and allow time for new methods of working to become established.

Transfer of training, whether from course to job or task to task, is a real problem. The recent research literature offers many useful ideas on how to increase the likelihood of transfer. However, it is necessary to decide what kind of transfer is desired before the learning activities are designed. Those activities which emphasize rehearsal of procedures may be inappropriate if transfer to a variety of job tasks is intended. In order to maximize the probability of transfer, it will be necessary to have post-learning support in place, and this usually implies the involvement of managers or colleagues.

If all these processes are to become organizational practice, the status of the training department may need to be reviewed and the policy clearly stated. This is, of course, a task for the organization as much as the training department, but the initiative may well have to come from the latter. Effective training implies a thorough understanding of the business plans and the organization's future objectives. Trainers will need to deal directly with line managers and thus gain their trust and respect. This will usually result from a track record of actually having helped to improve effectiveness. Evaluation is one way of increasing the contact between the training function and line managers. It is also the most likely method of establishing that training is helping to increase the effectiveness of parts of the organization.

PART THREE

How to evaluate changes due to training

Introduction

In Part Two, various ways of evaluating the process of training were discussed. The underlying theme was that the process should be designed not only to achieve changes in the way the trainees think or the ways in which they act, but also that these changes should result in greater effectiveness in the workplace.

It is, of course, necessary to use some form of measurement to assess whether the changes have actually taken place, and this is the focus of this part of the book. For clarity of presentation, a specific aspect of change—knowledge, skills, attitudes, etc.—will be selected when considering methods of measurement, but the changes achieved will be multifaceted, with many different aspects integrated. Learning affects the whole person and increases in knowledge or skills will usually result in different attitudes to some aspect of the work.

Organizational change occurs at many levels and takes many forms. Consequently, developing criteria by which changes can be evaluated may result in a range of indices. A good place to start is by establishing that learning has taken place at the individual level. This is one of the necessary conditions of those strategies of organizational change which focus on people. It cannot be assumed, however, that individual learning will lead to a change in effectiveness, and this will need to be evaluated in its own right.

First, techniques intended to measure changes in individual levels of knowledge, skills and attitudes will be described. Next, the criteria for evaluating increases in effectiveness at the individual, the team and the organizational level will be discussed. Finally, some aspects of comparing the costs of training with outcomes will be considered.

8 Measuring changes in knowledge

Levels of knowledge

All jobs require the holder to have some knowledge. What type of knowledge is required? How can this be analysed? It is helpful, in attempting to answer these questions, to have some framework in which to carry out the analysis. One which has proved to be useful is to describe the sort of knowledge required at three levels:

1 The basic level is that of isolated pieces of information—ability to recall simple lists or state simple rules, knowing a range of simple facts about the job area. This is often called *declarative* knowledge: information about 'what'. For instance, a counter clerk at the Post Office would need to know what forms have to be filled in and what documents produced in order to apply for a vehicle licence disc.

2 A higher level is to be able to arrange a good many of the pieces of information into procedures, how to do things, how to order sets of actions. This is often called *procedural* knowledge: information about 'how'. For instance, starting up a processing plant involves a series of actions which must be done in a certain sequence.

3 Higher still is the knowledge with which to analyse any particular situation for its key elements and thus to make a decision about whether procedure 'A' is more likely to be successful than (say) procedure 'D'. This is essentially the skill to be able to select the most appropriate procedure or method of doing something, given the nature of the problem, the organizational context, etc. This is often called *strategic* knowledge: information about 'which, when and why'. For instance, a social worker may have to decide whether a particular youngster's needs are best met by leaving him or her in the family of origin or by taking him or her into care, either by fostering or in a residential home.

This is a hierarchical set and it is not possible to achieve the higher levels without knowledge at the lower levels. The function of training could therefore be seen as:

● analysing what is required for satisfactory job performance at each of the three levels

- discovering what the trainees know at each level before they attend the training
- trying to close that gap
- communicating to the supervisor or manager to what extent the trainers are below satisfactory job performance levels at the end of training.

The three levels of knowledge have quite different implications for the training process. Isolated pieces of information can be quite easily transferred to large groups by lectures or by paper-based texts or by programmed packages. All of these methods are relatively inexpensive. Procedures too can be learned fairly cheaply by using checklists and prompts plus, perhaps, some supervised practice.

The implications of the third (analytic or strategic) level are quite different. If this is to be achieved, the trainees will have to practise in realistic situations and make decisions about what to do. As this is actually a simulation of some aspects of the job, it will be much more expensive to design and take much more time to run than the learning at the lower levels.

The implications for the sophistication of measurement of changes in knowledge are also different. It is relatively easy to test knowledge of isolated pieces of information and of procedures. This can be done by simple testing, where the answers can easily be seen to be right or wrong. At the analytic level, the solutions to the problems posed will often have a qualitative aspect to them. This will imply that a subject expert will have to scrutinize the solutions and decide which are acceptable and which are not. With highly developed simulations, these decisions are built in, but this is an extremely expensive process. For instance, flight simulators for airliners which allow the practice of a wide range of emergency procedures cost a minimum of £50 million each.

Testing knowledge

Open-ended questions

The traditional way of testing knowledge in our educational system is by use of the essay. Questions like: 'Discuss the extent to which the Triple Entente contributed to the outbreak of World War 1' are said to distinguish between those who know something about the area and those who do not. What such questions actually test is not so much what the student knows but how well he or she can assemble a logical argument on paper. This skill is important to success in the jobs of lecturers who set such questions, and in many other professions, but it is unimportant in many jobs. This form of testing, when applied to training, is usually inappropriate, not because of the open-ended nature of the question, but because it is often testing a skill which is irrelevant.

Short answer items

Open-ended questions can be asked to test knowledge of isolated pieces of information and procedures. They can sometimes be used to test powers of analysis. The questions should start with a verb like:

State	Calculate	Describe (in your own words)
List	Determine	Write (short reports)
Label	Define	

The answer expected should be short and some indication of length should be specified.

It is relatively easy to write questions of this type to measure trainees' knowledge of a particular topic. The marking of the answers may, however, pose some problems. Some of these are listed below:

1 Answers may vary but still be correct.
2 It is difficult to mark them consistently as the decision criterion correct/incorrect tends to drift over time.
3 A detailed marking guide is necessary.
4 The marking guide will often need some amendment after a few answers have been read in order to incorporate unforeseen alternatives.
5 Quite often people will disagree about whether a particular answer is correct. This implies that where there is more than one marker there will be problems of reliability.
6 It is necessary for the person marking the answers to be a subject expert and this may be an expensive use of such a person's time.

Objective test items

An alternative to testing by using open-ended questions is to ask the trainee to write one or two words, or select the correct alternative from a number offered. With these objective test items the rules for scoring are made absolutely clear so that the answer can be recognized as being right or wrong and can be marked so by someone who knows nothing about the subject area being tested.

This kind of question is very suitable for testing low levels on our hierarchy of knowledge, but it takes some ingenuity to write them for higher levels. This has led to a folklore that objective test items are only suitable for very trivial scraps of knowledge. This is not necessarily the case. The Open University, for instance, does a lot of course assessment by using objective tests and some of the items are certainly not testing recognition of simple facts. An example is the sort of question where understanding of a theory is being tested by asking which of a set of statements is consistent with the theory. Some of these questions test the ability to apply the theory in new situations, a procedure which is quite close to the 'analysis' level of knowledge.

Objective test items have the advantage over open-ended questions that they take less time to answer and the test can therefore cover a much wider area of the topic in the same time. They are also less likely to be testing the level of literacy of the candidates. They have the disadvantage of being much more difficult to write.

Multichoice questions

Multichoice questions consist of a stem and four or five alternative responses, and can be in the form of a statement or a question, for example:

Statement	Question
A tachometer indicates:	What does a tachometer indicate?
a Road speed	a Road speed
b Oil pressure	b Oil pressure
c Engine speed	c Engine speed
d Battery charge	d Battery charge

The trainee circles or crosses out the alternative selected; anyone with a marking brief can decide whether the answer is correct or not.

Simple guidelines are available for writing this kind of test item. Stems should:

- be clear and brief
- not include negatives
- not give clues by using key words which are repeated in the correct alternative answer.

Incorrect alternatives (usually called distractors) should:

- all be plausible
- all be incorrect
- be arranged in a random order so that the correct answer cannot be guessed because of its place in the sequence of alternatives.

General considerations are:

- Each item should test a concept which it is important for the trainee to know.
- No item should reveal the correct response to another item.
- The items should be grouped by type so that the instructions can be made simple.

True/false questions

Multichoice items are often difficult to write because sufficient plausible alternatives cannot be found. In this case, it is possible to use a specific form, the *true/false* item, for instance:

'*Filet mignon* is obtained from best end of mutton'   True/False

With this type of item there is a greater likelihood that only trivial information will be tested. There is also the possibility of giving clues by using words like 'never' or 'always' in the stem as these are usually false statements.

Correcting for guesswork It is clear that if a candidate is faced with a true/false test, knows nothing and guesses each item, he or she will score about 50 per cent. If it seems likely that some guessing is taking place, a guessing correction can be applied:

True score = Number of items correct − Number of items wrong

With multichoice items there is less likelihood of guessing in a random fashion. If necessary, this likelihood can be reduced by requesting that the candidates should not guess but leave questions unanswered when they have no idea what the answer is. It is also possible to use a guessing correction with the formula now becoming:

$$\text{True score} = \text{Number right} - \frac{\text{Number wrong}}{(\text{Number of alternatives} - 1)}$$

e.g. the candidate has 70 right, 21 wrong and has not attempted 9 on a multichoice test with 4 alternatives:

$$\text{True score} = 70 - \frac{21}{(4 - 1)}$$

$$= 70 - 7$$

$$= 63$$

The amount of guessing which is occurring is, in itself, an interesting measure of knowledge. People who have learned something and who are answering questions which are not ambiguous should not need to guess.

Objective test items need some drafting skill as well as knowledge of the area and they need to undergo some pilot testing to ensure that the trainees do not find them ambiguous. Test items that have worked particularly well should be collected to form a test battery for future occasions. A way of refining them and selecting them for an item bank is described in the 'Item analysis' part of Appendix 1.

Test results contain a good deal of information which can be of use in evaluating training. The mean (or average) mark tells us something about how difficult the test was for the trainees. Comparison of two sets of scores from different groups of trainees will give an indication of whether one group learned more than the other. If test results are to be used for evaluative purposes (or for feedback), the test will need to be reliable, i.e. to consistently measure what it is supposed to be measuring. These issues of comparing sets of scores and establishing the reliability of a test are discussed in Appendix 1, 'Analysing test scores'.

Gain ratios

When we looked at a framework for analysing types of knowledge required, it was suggested that training could be considered as an attempt to close the gap between present and desired levels of knowledge. From this statement it would appear to be logical to measure knowledge before as well as after training and thus estimate the gain. There are problems in doing this. The most obvious is that it may be a waste of valuable training time to establish that the trainees know virtually nothing at the beginning of the programme. It is also necessary to produce two similar but different tests, or the trainees will be alerted to the questions to be asked at the end of the programme and may concentrate on learning the answers to these particular questions rather than learning the principles which allow them to answer a range of similar questions.

There are some situations where it is worth while to pre-test as well as post-test knowledge. The gain ratio which can be calculated from this will give an estimate of the effectiveness of the programme. Using the formula:

$$\text{Gain ratio} = \frac{\text{Post-test score} - \text{Pre-test score}}{\text{Possible score} - \text{Pre-test score}} \times 100\%$$

a figure which takes values between 0 and 100 per cent will be obtained for each candidate. This represents how effective the programme was in teaching the particular individual what he or she needed to learn. The average gain ratio over a group of trainees gives a course effectiveness measure. As a guide one should expect an average gain ratio of about:

50 per cent with a good instructor and a good balance between input and practice
70 per cent or better with individualized instruction of programmed packages
30 per cent with short lectures followed by questions.

These figures are empirical, based on studies of actual gains made, and can probably be explained by the level of active learning involved in the three methods.

Poor levels of gain may also indicate that the trainees do not comprise a homogenous group. It is quite often the case that some know a good deal about the topic before training and some know virtually nothing. When this happens, the tutors will pitch the learning rate at a level which is too high for some and too low for others. If this is a serious problem it will be revealed because the gain ratios will tend to cluster into two groups: high for people whose pre-scores were low and low for the others or (vice versa). The implication here is that a pre-test could filter the candidates into two streams for more effective learning.

Organization of knowledge

Objective tests are best suited to testing the retention of declarative knowledge and sometimes they can be used early in a programme to discover gaps which may hinder the development of higher levels of knowledge. As learning advances, the trainees will focus less on isolated pieces of information and more on procedural knowledge. Concurrent with this will be the development of structures for organizing knowledge which will help with the present tasks and with anticipating future ones.

Subject experts have structures for organizing knowledge (mental maps) which are different from those used by learners. One way of assessing the gain in understanding achieved during the programme is to compare the mental maps which trainees are using with those of subject experts (usually the tutors). For instance, Goldsmith, Johnson and Acton (1991) identified 30 core concepts to be covered in the course. The students were presented with all possible pairs and required to judge the relatedness of the concepts using a seven-point scale. These structural representations were taken during weeks 1, 8 and 15 of the programme and compared with one produced by the course tutors. The mental maps of the students became more like that of the tutors as the course progressed, and the more closely an individual student's map matched that of the tutors, the better the student did in the final course tests ($r = 0.74$).

Assessment of knowledge at the strategic or analytic level will often include asking trainees about their level of awareness and understanding in order to estimate how they are organizing the knowledge which they have. For instance, asking them how they generate hypotheses about which procedures are more likely to succeed; asking them about how they test hypotheses and how they decide whether they are making progress; asking them about what sub-goals they have and how these link to the overall goal.

Following up knowledge-based programmes

Knowledge is actually taught in the belief that it is necessary for the job. It follows that the evaluation of knowledge gain is often not complete until the trainee has been followed back into the workplace to discover to what extent the knowledge is useful. This is, essentially, to check that the original analysis of what was required at each level is still an accurate reflection of the reality. The initial investigation can be done by using questionnaires, but it may also be necessary to follow some of these up by interviews. A suggested format for the questionnaire is given in Figure 8.1.

(The design of questionnaires to collect data for particular purposes is a skilled task. Some assistance with this is offered in Appendix 2, 'Designing questionnaires and analysing the data'.)

Topic (A detailed list of the areas covered on the programme)	How useful is knowledge of this for your job?			Have you used knowledge in this area since the course?			Have you had any difficulty in applying this?		
	Very	Quite	Not	Often	Seldom	Never	No	At first	Still
Topic 1									
Topic 2									
etc.									

Figure 8.1   *A questionnaire for following up knowledge-based programmes*

Where more than a third of respondents do not think that the knowledge is useful, or have not used it in six months following the training, the relevance of the topic should be reviewed. This is best done by interviewing a sample of people doing the job and their supervisors. Where people say that they 'still have difficulty' they should be asked to specify, as far as they can, what the nature of the difficulty is in the space provided on the back of the questionnaire form. It may be necessary, when these are examined, to seek further information about the precise nature of the difficulty. Again, this is easiest to do in interviews. Information on designing interviews for evaluative purposes is given in Appendix 3.

A fourth area might be investigated on the front of the questionnaire by asking, against relevant topics, whether the reference material supplied was adequate. Sometimes if good written material is prepared for courses the trainees can use this to help them after training and, where this is possible, the time spent on the topic during training can be reduced. It would certainly be worth asking them if this was the case. Places on off-the-job training are limited and expensive.

9 Measuring changes in levels of skills

Levels of skills

We used a hierarchical set of levels of knowledge to help with the planning of assessments before, during and after learning. A suggested set of levels for *skills* is given below:

1 The basic level with skills is *communication*, and for this it is necessary to be able to label things, to identify parts, to name the main assemblies of a machine, etc.

2 This level involves the ability to perform *simple procedures*, often with the use of instructions or notes. By simple procedures we mean things like changing the wheel on a car, where there is a sequence to follow but each part of the procedure involves only a very simple skill. As skill develops within this level, the behaviour becomes less error-prone and the individual steps become integrated and thought of as a single act. When the skill has developed, it should be flexible enough for the trainee to modify it to meet a variety of task situations. For instance, sales trainees can be confronted by an atypical customer.

3 This level is one of performing *skilled actions*. These often involve hand/eye coordination and learning them requires considerable practice. Examples are planing a piece of timber to the required size, or typing at 70 words a minute. With practice, it becomes possible to accomplish the task without conscious monitoring and this enables concurrent performance on additional tasks. For instance, as skill at car driving improves it is no longer necessary to be completely focused on changing gear; this can be done automatically and attention given to traffic conditions and conversation with a passenger. This is often called 'skill automaticity'.

4 A higher level of skill is that involved in *judging* whether a piece of skilled work is of acceptable quality; for instance, deciding whether a piece of finished metalwork is satisfactory or not.

The length of time spent in training and the sophistication of the testing situation will increase with increasing levels.

Testing levels of skills

Skills should usually be tested by practical tests unless the skill of being able to do something can be assumed from the ability to state the correct sequence of actions. Hands-on tests are expensive both in time and in wear to costly equipment. Sometimes it is possible to use an interview to ask the trainee to describe the steps necessary to complete a particular task. Sometimes listing the sequence is a rather different skill. For instance, I can state how to strip, clean and assemble the carburettor on my old tractor, but when I actually do it the carburettor doesn't work properly afterwards.

Tests of skills fall into two main types:

- The trainee is set a task (for example, to repair something) and the work is inspected at the end of the test period.
- The trainee is watched throughout the test so that the methods used can be assessed as well as the final product.

The first type of test is more economical in terms of the time spent by tutors or testers. The second is more flexible as the trainee who makes an error in the initial stages can be put back onto the correct path by the tester and thus demonstrate ability to carry out other parts of the task. Some tasks will require the second type of test because the result will not show how well the work has been carried out. Some kinds of welding, for instance, need to be watched during the process as the quality of weld will not be obvious from a surface inspection.

Observation is a flexible technique for collecting evaluative data. It has some similarities with interviewing in that it can be quite unstructured or be supported by a very detailed schedule. Information about observing as an evaluative technique can be found in Appendix 4.

Some written tests can also be practical tests. The 'in-tray' type of test which is often used in assessment centres is an example. The problems set are those likely to arise in the job, and the close relationship between the testing situation and the reality of the job make it a very good predictor of job success. This is generally true of practical tests as they can usually simulate job conditions much more accurately than tests of knowledge.

Practical tests have the disadvantage of being expensive because of the time required to supervise them and also because they often tie up expensive equipment. It is also more difficult to mark them reliably as the standards used will usually vary with different testers. Just how serious this is can be demonstrated by a simple exercise using electrical three-pin plugs. Six plugs are wired up to three-core cable with one wired correctly and the others with defects, say:

a wired correctly

b live lead to neutral

c too much bare wire

d wrong lead to earth

e loose cable retainer bar

f one loose connection

A number of testers are asked to mark the finished work (and given no information on standards or mark scales). Wiring such plugs is something that most people do regularly as electrical equipment is often sold (in the UK) without a plug. However, the standards which people find acceptable vary. On a number of occasions when we have used this exercise, we have found that some will accept plug C and/or E, some will even accept D. Most will mark out of 5 or 10 and a few will mark on a pass/fail basis.

This emphasizes the general rule that detailed marking guides are necessary for practical tests. In addition, where more than one examiner is used, the marks should be compared and standardized on a few examples of work so that critical aspects of judgement can be agreed.

The same is true of performance tests. In this case it is often worth video recording a few attempts at the skill and asking the testers to develop a marking schedule. Figure 9.1 shows a simple schedule developed by this process.

Profiling skills

The use of the four levels of skill, and estimating at each level what adequate job performance means, allows the identification of individual needs for training. Effective training will also require some estimate of what the trainees are able to do before training. Often this can be assumed to be very little, but sometimes it is worth testing.

A large UK company which employs some hundreds of fitters to carry out servicing of central heating systems in homes was faced with the necessity of improving the quality of this service because of increasing competition. An off-job programme of three one-week modules was designed to cover the skills necessary to carry out the work. All the fitters were tested using fault-finding exercises mounted on boards which represented the main types of heating system. The ways in which the fitters attempted these simple diagnostic tests were used to decide how many of the one-week modules each should attend. It was then possible to plan a programme of training courses which accurately met the skills needs across the population of fitters.

Serial	Sub-tasks	YES	NO
1	Stop on hard, level surface		
2	Apply handbrake		*
3	Engage low gear		*
4	Chocks or bricks in front and behind wheels		*
5	Remove tools and spare wheel		
6	Check tyre pressure of spare and adjust if necessary		
7	Place jack under chassis nearest to wheel to be changed		
8	Loosen wheel nuts		
9	Jack up wheel approximately 1″ from ground		
10	Remove nuts—top nut last		
11	Remove wheel		
12	Place spare wheel on hub		
13	Secure top nut first		*
14	Tighten all nuts, diagonally		
15	Lower Jack—wheel on ground		
16	Tighten nuts fully		*
17	Place spare wheel in carrier		
18	Clean tools		
19	Replace tools		
20	Question student on subsequent check (nuts to be checked at next inspection)		
	*These are critical tasks as they involve safety and failure to observe them will result in a failure of the test.	Result PASS/FAIL	

Figure 9.1 *Changing a wheel: marking schedule*

Profiling is widely used in education as a method of recording how far students have developed along a particular path. It can also be used in a training context for assessing where trainees are at present and where they should aim to be at the end of training. City and Guilds of London use a format of five attainment levels, each defined by a behavioural anchor, for example:

Using equipment	Can use equipment safely to perform a sequence of tasks after demonstration	Can select and use suitable equipment and materials for the job	Can set up and use equipment to produce work to standard	Can identify and remedy common faults in equipment
	20 May 95		30 Jun 95	

A discussion takes place between the trainee and the tutor and the category which is thought to be most relevant is identified. This box is dated. A second date is entered into one of the boxes to the right which is thus identified as the next objective and the date at which achievement of this will be reviewed.

This process of identifying benchmarks for skills and then regularly checking progress against them could be widely used in skills training. The book by Rackham and Morgan (1977), which we mentioned when discussing ways of structuring learning events (page 59), advocates the use of just such a process in the training of interpersonal skills.

The assessment centre has been used for many years as a method of selecting employees for promotion. The individuals being assessed are given a series of exercises which are thought typical of the work at the next level of seniority. For a typical management assessment centre there would be some evaluation of skills like communication, planning and organizing, analysis, judgement and delegation. There might also be some assessment of abilities like business sense or generation of creative ideas. Senior managers in the organization would be trained to use detailed observation categories and asked to do the assessment. The process can take anything from half a day to three days.

More recently, assessment centres have been used for the identification of development needs. The exercises are again based upon the analysis of what is required for success at the next level of seniority and the assessment is done in a similar way. The purpose is different as the areas which are identified as being weak are made the basis of individual development programmes. The effectiveness of these programmes can be assessed by attendance at a second assessment centre after an interval of (say) one year. The candidates are again assessed and improvements noted.

Another method of using the assessment centre as an evaluative tool was reported by Byham (1982). Managers who had completed four weeks of training in various management skills took a series of tests in an assessment centre together with a similar number who had not yet been trained. The two groups were matched for level in the organization, education and experience. The assessors were, of course, unaware of who had been trained and who had not. It was found that the group which had been trained performed better than the untrained group on all of the dimensions. They scored about 40 per cent better on skills like oral communication, problem analysis, judgement and delegation. They scored about 20 per cent better on dimensions like leadership and decisiveness.

Following up skills-based programmes

Technical skills which have been properly learned transfer easily to the workplace. If they have been learned to the higher end of level 2 they should generalize to the varying conditions found in the work. If they have been learned to automaticity, level 3, they should be maintained over long periods with little further practice. It is possible to assess whether the automaticity level has been reached by requiring performance of the skill under two conditions—one with many distractions and one with few. If the learners have reached the level of automaticity, there should be little difference between the two performances, with speed and accuracy of operation being similar.

The reason for following up skills training of this type is not so much to check on transfer as to ensure that the training time is being used effectively, i.e. to train those skills which are actually required and to train them only to the level necessary. The principal task is to check that the original needs analysis was correct. The questions which need answering include:

- Could they have easily learned the skill on the job?
- Do they do it often enough to make it worth while learning?
- Are the levels right or do they need further development on the job?
- Is that part of the job still done that way or are the trainers out of date?

Follow-up questionnaires of the type in Figure 9.2 will provide a good deal of the information necessary. These should be sent to the participants some time after training when they have had an opportunity to experience the range of the job, usually between three months and a year depending upon the complexity of the work.

Tasks	How often?			Is it difficult?*		
Since the course have you had to:	Never	Sometimes	Often	Never	At first	Still
Diagnose mechanical faults in						
Repair or assist the repair of						
Use						
Supervise someone using						
etc.						

* If it is still difficult, please specify the reasons in the blank spaces on the back of this page.

Figure 9.2 *A follow-up questionnaire for skills-based courses*

In the following-up of skills training it will almost certainly be necessary to contact the managers, and this can also be done using a questionnaire. An example is offered in Figure 9.3.

Tasks	Is it necessary for him/her to do this?	Can he/she do it to your satisfaction?			Would you rather have trained him/her to do this yourself?
The trainee has been taught to:	Yes No	Yes, without supervision	Yes, with supervision	No	Yes No
Diagnose mechanical faults in					
Repair or assist the repair of					
Use					
Supervise someone using					
etc.					
etc.					

Figure 9.3 *A follow-up questionnaire for supervisors*

It is also useful to have an open-ended 'remarks' column on the right.

It may be necessary to interview a sample of participants and their managers to discuss details of why things are difficult or why some performances are not up to standard. This might be done directly or by telephone. Sometimes managers want all ex-trainees to be able to do everything with a high degree of skill. It will rarely be possible or economic to train to that level off-job and a face-to-face discussion may be necessary to establish where the responsibility of the trainers finishes and that of the manager starts. Part of the responsibility for developing to operational standards must usually be taken by the manager, except in those rare situations where this is not possible (e.g. landing space capsules on the moon and then driving moon buggies).

10 Changes in attitudes and behaviour

Attitude change versus behaviour change

The distinction between skills and attitudes is an important one. Indeed, failure to clarify the difference between skills training and attitude change can often result in confusion. This is not to suggest that the two are incompatible but rather that trainers need to decide which aspects of their programmes are addressed to skills and which to attitudes. In this way the process of evaluation can be designed to look at one aspect separately from the other and to give appropriate feedback.

Let us consider a working definition which will clarify this important distinction. An attitude is a tendency or a predisposition to behave in certain ways in particular situations, whereas a skill is an ability to do something well. Attitudes can be measured directly, but are usually inferred from the things which people say or are seen to do. Changing someone's attitude to something may well change what they say or do, but this will not necessarily follow. People behave in ways which they believe to be appropriate to the situation in which they find themselves so that other variables in the present situation may be more powerful than attitudes.

Reactions to programmes

The most common method of evaluating attitudes is that of measuring reactions to the programme itself. Indeed, many trainers argue that *the* essential part of the evaluation process is to measure these reactions. That, whatever else is done, it is important to discover how participants feel about the programme they have attended.

Most evaluation is done at this 'reaction' level. In the USA, Ralphs and Stephan (1986) found that 86 per cent of the Fortune 500 companies 'usually' evaluated their courses by means of evaluation forms filled in by learners at the end of the course, whereas only 12 per cent 'usually' used business data records. The study 'Training in Britain' (1989) carried out for the Training Agency was a survey of a large number of organizations, responsible for some 80 per cent of the employed workforce in the UK. The results showed that, in 1986/87, 90 per cent of the organizations in the survey used the reactions level of evaluation, but only 19 per cent attempted any evaluation in terms of benefit to the organization.

Perhaps an assumption is being made that favourable reactions imply useful learning or will predict changes in behaviour or higher levels of effectiveness. There is not much evidence to support this. The survey carried out by Alliger and Janak (1989) found 12 published articles in which attempts had been made to correlate levels of reaction with amount of learning or changes in work behaviour or levels of effectiveness. There are problems in generalizing from such a small data set, but, in the only studies published, there was no relationship between reaction measures and other criteria; *good* reactions did not predict learning or behaviour change or increased effectiveness any better than *poor* reactions. I would suggest that this implies that one should be wary of using only the reactions level when evaluating training events.

A further problem with evaluation at the reaction level is that it may be just measuring enjoyment, i.e. assessing training on the basis of its entertainment value. It may be necessary to make the programme interesting or challenging to stimulate motivation, but enjoyment *per se* may not be one of the important objectives. Evaluation is essentially an information-gathering process and it is important to write down, before any methods are decided, why the information is being collected and what use will be made of it. This should influence the questions asked and the format in which they are posed. The issuing of a two-page questionnaire towards the end of a programme has, in many organizations, become a ritual expected both by trainees and trainers. There are better ways of assessing the quality of the training.

Learning reviews

The first method which I would like to suggest is the discussion of the usefulness of the learning at stages during the event. For instance, in a five-day workshop, it is often informative to ask the participants at the end of the day to write down anything they have learned during the day that they think might be particularly *useful* for their work. Allow them some 15 minutes for this and then ask them to share with the group how they think they might apply the learning. The tutor gains a good deal of feedback about their understanding and the likelihood of transfer of learning. The participants are also helped to focus on utility, and the sheets produced at the end of each day can form the basis of an action planning session near the end of the workshop. It is also possible for the tutor to collect such sheets, carry out some analysis of them during the evening and use the summary of learning as a start point for the next day.

An alternative, which might be suitable for a residential programme, is for the tutor to carry out short, informal interviews with the delegates during the evenings. Questions can be posed about specific objectives in attending, what they have found particularly useful, what hasn't gone well for them, what they would like to spend more or less time on, etc.

The review which is most common occurs at the end of the learning event. The group is brought together and asked for comments about the content, the process and the administration. My experience is that these reviews are often meaningless rituals; some participants feel obliged to be polite and some feel that they ought to criticize something, while others say nothing. The key variable is not the quality of the programme but the personalities of the participants. Some of the problems can be overcome by splitting into small groups and reporting back to the large group, but this tends to extend the review when many are keen to be on their way home. A further criticism I would have is that the information gathered may be of little use. The end of the event is actually too late for purposes of adjusting the process or content to suit the particular group of participants, and the next run of the event will be with different people who will usually have rather different needs and objectives.

Behaviour analysis

Observation of the participants and analysis of their behaviour can also be a useful method of evaluating how well an event is progressing. If this is to be a reliable method, some fairly simple and objective system of categorizing behaviours will be necessary.

One such method has been suggested by Sanderson, James and Seidler (1989). The basic premise of their work is that verbalizations used by people about the skills which they are learning will change during training and these changes can be used to assess progress. The seven categories offered are given below:

1 *Contingency*. Used when a trainee expresses a relationship between two objects, e.g. the similarity between two safety devices.
2 *Identification*. The detection or identification of symptoms, but without any verbalization about meaning or implication.
3 *Interpretation*. Interpreting information as when someone applies general rules to a particular situation.
4 *Statement of action*. Verbalizations of short-term intentions or desires about the need to examine something or to carry out another action.
5 *Goal/intention*. Longer-range expressions of something akin to strategy, often based upon previous experience.
6 *Speculation/irrational statements*. Statements which do not follow logically from the information currently available.
7 *Questions*. Questions concerning the training system or some aspect of the work being tackled.

Changes in the nature of the verbalizations during training may be an important indicator of the effectiveness of the training. One might expect that verbalizations of identifications, interpretations and contingencies which were both correct and relevant would increase during training. One might also expect increases in statements concerning goals and intentions which were correct. Conversely, the frequency of speculations should decrease as a consequence of training.

For interpersonal skills programmes, a more suitable set of categories is that developed by Rackham and Morgan (1977). These are shown in Figure 10.1. These categories are intended to provide a vocabulary for communicating frequencies of doing things and thus act as an aid to providing accurate feedback which the recipient can understand. Important categories are selected from critical incident studies of the kind of work to be learned. Thus, where the job is one of taking telephone bookings, the categories thought to be important to good performance might include:

a high rate of

- seeking information—proposals, solutions to problems, etc.
- testing understanding
- summarizing

and a low rate of

- blocking/difficulty stating.

The frequency with which the operatives show these behaviours in early, practice interviews is fed back to them and discussed. They then have clear benchmarks against which to measure progress. The best place to do this behaviour tracking is, of course, in actual job situations, but it can also be used during off-job training.

End-of-event questionnaires

The most popular form of evaluation is the issue of a questionnaire during or at the end of the programme. This is usually justified as providing feedback for the tutors so that they can improve future courses. Some summary of the ratings is often used by training managers to monitor the quality of the programme.

I would again emphasize that it is important to decide what the information is to be used for before designing the questionnaire. Questions like:

How would you rate the course overall? Poor 1 2 3 4 5 Excellent

Did the course meet your objectives? Not at all 1 2 3 4 5 Totally

are very common, but they don't produce information which is specific enough to produce useful feedback for tutors. If this is the intention, a more useful format is that shown in Figure 10.2.

Proposing behaviour which puts forward a new concept, suggestion of course of action (and is actionable).

Building behaviour which extends or develops a proposal which has been made by another person (and is actionable).

Supporting behaviour which involves a conscious and direct declaration of support or agreement with another person or concepts.

Disagreeing behaviour which involves a conscious, direct and reasoned declaration of difference of opinion, or criticism of another person's concepts.

Defending/attacking behaviour which attacks another person or defensively strengthens an individual's own position. Defending/attacking behaviours usually involve overt value judgements and often contain emotional overtones.

Blocking/difficulty stating behaviour which places a difficulty or block in the path of a proposal or concept without offering any alternative proposal and without offering a reasoned statement of disagreement. Blocking/difficulty stating behaviour therefore tends to be rather bald, e.g. 'It won't work,' or 'We couldn't possibly accept that'.

Open behaviour which exposes the individual who makes it to risk of ridicule or loss of status. This behaviour may be considered as the opposite of defending/attacking. Included within this category are admissions of mistakes or inadequacies provided that these are made in a non-defensive manner.

Testing understanding behaviour which seeks to establish whether or not an earlier contribution has been understood.

Summarizing behaviour which summarizes, or otherwise restates in a compact form, the content of previous discussions or considerations.

Seeking information behaviour which seeks facts, opinions or clarification from another individual or individuals.

Giving information behaviour which offers facts, opinions or clarification to other individuals.

Shutting out behaviour which excludes, or attempts to exclude, another group member (e.g. interrupting, talking over).

Bringing in behaviour which is a direct and positive attempt to involve another group member.

Figure 10.1 *Categories of behaviour*
(*Source: Rackham and Morgan, 1977, Figure 2.2, page 31*)

In columns 'b' and 'c' encircle the number which in your opinion is the most appropriate according to the following scales:

	(b)			(c)	
Almost the information was new	1 2 3 4 5	Told me little that I didn't know already	Presentation needs no improvement	1 2 3 4 5	Presentation needs much improvement

In the remaining columns please tick (√) as appropriate

Topic	New information	Presentation	Time			This was difficult
			More	Less	Right	
a	b	c	d	e	f	g
Questionnaire/ design I	1 2 3 4 5	1 2 3 4 5				
Questionnaire/ design II (prc)		1 2 3 4 5				
Interviewing I	1 2 3 4 5	1 2 3 4 5				
Interviewing practice		1 2 3 4 5				

Figure 10.2 *End-of-course questionnaire*

The respondents should be encouraged to make open-ended comments on the back of the form. Any expression of 'difficulty' should be followed up to discover the source. To obtain the maximum useful information, such a questionnaire should be issued at the beginning of the programme and filled in by stages. It would also be worth while, in a programme which lasts longer than one week, to collect the forms at the end of each week and review them before fine-tuning the next week's work. It is likely that more open and honest comments and ratings will be obtained if the respondents are allowed to remain anonymous, although this does sometimes make it difficult to follow up and probe some of the 'this was difficult' remarks.

With any one particular session, more detailed feedback might be required, for instance:

- What is your overall reaction to the session on ...   Very good/Good/Fair/Poor
- Will you be able to use the material (or skill) in your job?   Frequently/Sometimes/Rarely/ Unlikely

- What did you think of the
  presentation of the session?   Very good/Good/Fair/Poor
- How do you think the session   _____
  could be improved?   _____

Sometimes the intention is to obtain more detail on rating the tutors. Something like Figure 10.3 should provide useful information:

Name of tutor _____   Title of session _____

                        Yes/No   Comments

Maintained a good pace
Kept to the subject
Knowledgeable
Enthusiastic
Created interest
Involved the group

Figure 10.3 *Rating a tutor*

A more detailed schedule, designed for observation of a trainer, is given in Appendix 4 on page 174.

It may also be useful to offer open-ended questions in the end-of-course questionnaire, for instance:

- What are the three best things about this course?
- What are the three worst things about this course?
- What three changes should be made to the course?
- What aspects of the process helped you to learn?
- What aspects hindered your learning?

It does, however, take some time for them to write answers to such questions and for the tutors to analyse and summarize the information collected. Again, I would suggest that one should consider how the information will be used. It may, for instance, be difficult to generalize, from the opinions of the present course on such questions as these, to the wishes of the next set of participants.

I have fewer reservations about the use of questionnaires when collecting information about external courses. It is difficult to monitor what is happening during the programme and reports on the course will usually include a questionnaire to examine the utility and relevance of what was done as well as the administration, accommodation, etc.

Attitude training

The process of attitude training has four main stages:

1 Identify desirable attitudes which are expected to lead to some improvement, usually of culture or climate, in some part of the organization. The attitudes identified are usually fairly general; things like: positive management; consideration for subordinates; openness and trust in the workplace; being less prescriptive and more likely to delegate responsibility.

2 Assess where the participants are with respect to the desired attitude. This is usually done by self-analysis, often with an inventory. The participants' perceptions of their 'normal' work behaviour are classified and some categories are shown to differ from the ideal.

3 Convince the participants of the value of the desired attitudes, by giving examples, models or counselling. This is reinforced by allowing them to experience some success in experiential learning, perhaps by role plays.

4 If the training is done well, the participants accept the new attitude and return to work. Here it is expected that they will display behaviour consistent with the new attitude.

As attitudes are measured or discussed early in the programme, it is possible to re-assess them towards the end and show changes in the expected direction. As well as direction, attitude strength can be assessed. How strongly they hold their views, how concerned they are about the issue and how likely they are to change their minds when they return to normal work routine, are all indicators of how likely it is that the attitude change will persist and transfer. Useful sources of inventories which may be used to assess attitudes early and late in the programme can be found in the book by Henerson, Morris and Fitzgibbon (1978) and also that by Cook *et al* (1981). The inventories will seldom be exactly what is required, but the formats can be used to build up something specific for a particular programme.

Semantic differentials

A simple method of checking whether there has been a change of attitude, and in what direction, is to use a semantic differential of the type shown in Figure 10.4. The participants are asked to think about a particular concept, say 'evaluation of training' or 'participative management', and to mark on each seven-point scale where their opinion lies. The opinions of the group are usually summarized by frequencies or average to give some feel of what their overall attitude is to the concept.

The exercise is repeated near the end of the programme and any changes in attitude can be identified. The technique is neutral with respect to the direction of the changes. The trainers should be able to assess whether a change on any particular dimension is positive and this should, of course, be related to the objectives of the programme. It is

The concept of participative management is:

Valuable	1	2	3	4	5	6	7	Worthless
Sincere	1	2	3	4	5	6	7	Insincere
Strong	1	2	3	4	5	6	7	Weak
Relaxed	1	2	3	4	5	6	7	Tense
Active	1	2	3	4	5	6	7	Passive
Warm	1	2	3	4	5	6	7	Cold
Fast	1	2	3	4	5	6	7	Slow

Figure 10.4 *A semantic differential*

also possible to measure whether the change is a significant one in the statistical sense, i.e. whether it is unlikely to have arisen by chance, by using a simple Chi-squared technique. Examples of how to do this can be found in Appendix 2.

Repertory grid

A more rigorous method of finding out what people's attitudes are towards a particular concept is to use a repertory grid. This technique asks the person whose attitudes are being investigated to consider a number of examples of the concept and to say what criteria he or she would use to distinguish between them. This is usually done in interviews but can be done with groups. For our purpose of evaluating change due to a programme, the group method will usually be more practical, as a one-hour interview with each individual separately is likely to involve too much time.

An example of the group method should help to clarify the procedure. Suppose we are about to start on a programme of interpersonal skills training with a group of junior managers. The starting point for the programme is to try to discover what their concepts of good interpersonal skills are. It should then be possible to develop a programme to start from this baseline and move the managers' views closer to those which are thought valuable within the organization.

Using a group rep-grid technique, each participant is asked to write down the names of six managers with whom he or she has worked: two who are thought to have very good interpersonal skills, two who are thought to be poor in this area and two who are in between. No attempt is made by the tutors to explain what they mean by interpersonal skills, as all the ideas must come from the participants. Each name is then written onto a small piece of paper, these are shuffled and then coded A, B, C, D, E and F.

They are now asked to draw out A, B and C from the six and think about what these three might do in work situations where interpersonal skills are involved. What is it that two of them might do that is similar? What is it that one might do that the other two would probably not do? In this way they select a pair who are likely to behave in a similar way and a single who would behave quite differently from the three labelled A, B and C. Each then writes down the pair description on the left of a prepared form as below.

Triad selection

Pair description	A	B	C	D	E	F	Single description
Supportive		*	*	*			Not supportive

Quite often these are obviously opposite statements, but this is not always the case.

Next they draw the papers labelled D, E and F from the six and repeat the process of deciding what two of them would do that makes their behaviour alike and what the other one would do that would be different. For instance:

Selection

Pair description	A	B	C	D	E	F	Single description
Listens to what I have to say				*	*	*	Preconceived ideas

It is important to supervise this and to ensure that the descriptions which are being written down are about what managers do rather than personality traits. Quite often the trainees will want to write down things like, 'warm personality'. Statements like this are at too high a level of generality to help us decide what needs to be learned in order to demonstrate 'warmth'.

The procedure is repeated until they have written down a number of contrasts by comparing different combinations of managers. Drawing three from six in ten ways, say ABC, DEF, ACF, BDE, ADF, BEF, CDF, ABE, BCD, ACE, will ensure that each manager is entered into the comparisons six times and should give enough information on how each participant distinguishes between categories of interpersonal skill.

The contrasts are not, so far, related to judgements about what the participants think represents good practice. This can be elicited in interviews, but it is also possible to do it by a simple scoring process. On each line the participants score their contrasts on a 1 to 6 scale by giving the manager who is most like the pair description a 1 and the one who is most like the single description a 6. Then 2 and 5 are allocated to the next most like and so on with 3 and 4. For instance, if manager C is most supportive and manager A least supportive we might have:

Pair description	A	B	C	D	E	F	Single description
Supportive	*	*	*				Not supportive
	6	2	1	3	4	5	
Listens to what				*	*	*	Preconceived ideas
I have to say	5	3	2	1	4	6	

Some will want to use shared rankings (equal 3, etc.), but they should not be allowed to do this.

When they have scored all ten contrasts, these scores can be correlated with their view of good interpersonal skills. This is done by each of them ranking the six managers who make up the A to F using 1 for best and 6 for worst at interpersonal skills. These numbers are written down on a separate piece of paper, say:

	A	B	C	D	E	F
Overall effectiveness	6	3	2	1	4	5

The ranking on overall effectiveness is now correlated with that on each of the contrasts, for example:

Pair	A	B	C	D	E	F	Single
Supportive	6	2	1	3	4	5	Non-supportive
Overall	6	3	2	1	4	5	
Differences	0	1	1	2	0	0 = 4	

Pair	A	B	C	D	E	F	Single
Listens	5	3	2	1	4	6	Preconceived ideas
Overall	6	3	2	1	4	5	
Differences	1	0	0	0	0	1 = 2	

The differences in ranks are summed, regardless of sign, to give a score. The signs are ignored as it is the size of the difference which is important. Where the resulting score is small, i.e. 0 or 2, the description in the contrasts is defining what the participant means by good interpersonal skills. Because of the method of scoring, high scores will result when the positive description is on the right (i.e. the single description). Thus the highest possible scores (18 and 16) are also defining what the participant means by good interpersonal skills. (It is usually worth checking the arithmetic at this stage. There are six pairs and therefore all of the scores should be even numbers; those people who have odd numbers should recalculate the differences.) Contrasts which have scores of between 4 and 12 are ways in which managers differ, but are not closely related to the concept of good interpersonal skills (in the minds of the participants). Contrasts which are not opposites will seldom correlate highly with the overall criterion. This is because they are not on a linear dimension which the theory of correlation requires. For our purposes this is not really a problem as we wish to use only those contrasts which are very close to the overall criterion.

The contrasts which have scored 0 or 2 or 16 or 18 can be examined with individuals to draw out what, for each of them, is the definition of good interpersonal skills. With a group these contrasts can be collected and displayed to give an introduction to the programme. One of our groups produced a list which included the following:

Gets the job done but with concern	—	Self-centred
Treats people as individuals	—	Stereotypes people
Encourages development	—	Does not encourage development
Adult reactions	—	Childish
Talks through problems with me	—	Unable to see my difficulties
Listens but doesn't do anything	—	Listens and then acts
Lets people have some discretion	—	Closely monitors

Some personality traits have slipped in here, and these contrasts need further expansion. What was meant by 'adult reactions' and what behaviour would be classified as 'childish'? are questions that would need to be asked. Discussing types of behaviour like this gave a good lead into talking about interpersonal skills and thus into the main topic for the week.

This group procedure takes about one and a half hours, but it gives a good feel for the attitudes that the participants have towards the concept at the beginning of the programme. It also introduces the area as it requires them to think carefully about the subject and clarifies what they as individuals believe. Sometimes this actually confronts them with attitudes which they did not expect. A group of managers in the National Health Service who were attending a management course were asked to produce a set of contrasts which would distinguish between a good and a bad hospital patient. It did not surprise us, but it did them, to find that many produced a picture of a good patient as someone who lay still and didn't complain.

Towards the end of the training the procedure above can be repeated and the results compared. As they will now be familiar with the process, the second attempt will take much less time— perhaps 45 minutes. Changes can be assessed in a number of ways:

- An improvement in the number of contrasts scoring 0 or 2 or 16 or 18. At the beginning most of them will only have a few such contrasts as their views about the concept are rather diffuse. At the end they should be much more focused on the area which has been discussed.
- There should be fewer personality traits and more descriptions of what people do.
- Many of the constructs being used should be close to those offered by the tutors, i.e. identifiable from the objectives of the programme.

The repertory grid is a sophisticated technique with many variations to suit particular situations. An interesting use of it was described by Valerie Fournier (1994), of the University of St Andrews. Graduates were asked to generate constructs on a number of elements—actual self, ideal self, line manager, competent person, disliked colleague, etc.—when they were two weeks into their first job. The process was repeated after six months and again after nine months. Analysis of the grids showed changes in the cognitive maps being used and these showed less likelihood to trust managers and decreasing hope that the organization would offer interesting work over the period of the study.

Many organizations have used rep-grids to define the differences between successful and less successful senior managers and thus provided a basis for management appraisal and development through assessment centres. Some companies use it for customer service training. Other applications within organizational contexts can be found in Stewart and Stewart (1981). Some of the more complicated methods require computer analysis of the grids, but, for our purposes in evaluating training, simple procedures which require only basic analysis like that described above will suffice.

Following up attitude and behaviour change

It is possible to follow up changes in attitudes back to the workplace to discover to what extent they have been maintained, but it is doubtful whether this will actually produce useful information. One is still left with the assumption that changes in attitude imply changes in behaviour at work. An approach which seems more likely to help with evaluation is through the use of behaviour scales to measure changes in the ways in which things are done. If the new behaviours are found to be effective in solving work problems, the individuals should recognize their value and internalize the attitudes which are congruent with them (Goldstein and Sorcher, 1974).

Behaviour scales

The basic rationale of using behaviour scales is that they can make explicit what changes are expected to result from training and give some estimate of whether they are actually occurring.

One way of doing this is to make explicit which parts of the annual appraisal categories will be likely to change as a result of the programme. Figure 10.5 offers an example taken from a course in 'Consulting Skills'. The aspect of 'Interpersonal skills' has been extracted from the annual appraisal form and is used to communicate to the candidate and his or her employing manager which categories of behaviour are the target of the programme.

Interpersonal skills: Usually involves the establishing of sound, straight forward and fruitful relationships with people

---

● The ability to look at a situation from the other person's point of view and balance it against one's own perceptions	Strong/Adequate/Weak
● The ability to influence others	S/A/W
● The ability to appreciate how another person feels empathy	S/A/W
● The ability to handle conflict while maintaining a good relationship	S/A/W
● The ability to convey ideas and agreements with clarity	S/A/W

Figure 10.5 *A behaviour scale based on an appraisal form*

During the programme the participant keeps a log of perceived improvements in these areas, and this is a tracking of attitude change as much as anything. The format also gives a clear rationale for the employing manager to make pre- and post-training comparisons in terms which are well understood within the company. It can thus be used in evaluating behaviour change at work.

It is also possible to take the objectives of the programme and translate them into statements of what people are more likely to do after the programme. Two examples are given in Figure 10.6, one from a programme on 'Positive Management' and the other about 'Consideration' as part of a management course.

The rationale is again that of making explicit what changes in behaviour are expected. The format can be used before and after by the candidates themselves and by their managers to give estimates of attitude and behaviour changes.

The people who are best able to assess the behaviour of managers are their staff, and it is sometimes possible to use their opinions to measure changes. For instance, in an attempt to change an autocratic to a more consultative style of management (Bramley, 1994), staff opinions of the management style of 13 of the 60 heads of department in a company were collected. The 13 middle managers were each given a summary of their staff's views, expressed as (anonymous) answers to questions like those in Figure 10.7.

Positive management	Never 0–19	Seldom 20–39	Sometimes 40–59	Generally 60–79	Always 80–100%
1 Thinks ahead and develops plans rather than constantly clearing up problems	☐	☐	☐	☐	☐
2 Thinks in terms of objectives rather than vague generalizations and makes them both clear and realistic	☐	☐	☐	☐	☐
3 Takes decisions rather than procrastinating or passing problems up to the next level	☐	☐	☐	☐	☐
4 Coordinates the group's activities and checks on progress to achieve objectives	☐	☐	☐	☐	☐
5 Deals with subordinates as individuals and makes each accountable for a specific set of responsibilities	☐	☐	☐	☐	☐

etc. (The scale will need to be at least 10 items long to give good reliability)

or **Consideration**	Never	Seldom	Sometimes	Generally	Always
1 Welcomes new ideas and alternatives	☐	☐	☐	☐	☐
2 Gets the approval of subordinates on important matters before going ahead	☐	☐	☐	☐	☐
3 Expresses appreciation personally to people who do a good job	☐	☐	☐	☐	☐
4 Makes opportunities to develop people as individuals	☐	☐	☐	☐	☐
5 Knows when individuals have problems, is helpful and supportive	☐	☐	☐	☐	☐

etc. (again, at least 10 items)
Organizational constraints might make it impossible, but the people best qualified to give this sort of information are subordinates!

Figure 10.6 *Scales for changes in behaviour*

1	Jointly sets clear tasks and targets with you	1	2	3	4	5
2	Jointly reviews progress on tasks and targets at timely intervals	1	2	3	4	5
3	Lets you know exactly what is expected of you	1	2	3	4	5
4	Delegates sufficient authority and responsibility to you	1	2	3	4	5
5	Actively supports and promotes your ideas	1	2	3	4	5
6	Demonstrates concern about your development	1	2	3	4	5
7	Coaches and guides effectively	1	2	3	4	5
8	Is committed to team building	1	2	3	4	5
9	Encourages good relationships	1	2	3	4	5
10	Creates a trusting environment	1	2	3	4	5
11	Is a good listener	1	2	3	4	5
12	Shows genuine interest in you and your work	1	2	3	4	5

Scoring: 1 = agree, 2 = tend to agree,
3 = neither agree nor disagree,
4 = tend to disagree, 5 = disagree

Figure 10.7 *Subordinate feedback items*

The middle managers discussed this feedback with the consultant and signed learning contracts to attempt to improve in areas where they felt it would be worth while. These learning contracts, supported by training opportunities in 'Setting joint targets' and 'How to get the best out of group meetings', proved to be effective in achieving changes in behaviour. One year later, the opinions of staff were collected again and the contrast is shown in Figure 10.8 (the calculation of Chi-square is described in Appendix 2).

In 1992 more of the 190 junior managers in the survey chose the 'agree' or 'tend to agree' categories than was the case in 1991. The changes were statistically significant for all 12 questions shown in Figure 10.8. The implication of this is that a significant change in the behaviour of the middle managers (departmental heads) had taken place. These were not the only questions asked; other questions about 'decisiveness' and 'dealing with unsatisfactory performance' showed no changes year on year. The scheme was offered to other middle managers, on a voluntary basis, and to date some 30 more middle managers have taken advantage of it. The results have been similar to those obtained with the 13 in the original pilot scheme.

		1	2	3	4	5	Chi-square
1	Jointly sets targets	10/29	33/43	32/18	23/10	2/0	21.62***
2	Jointly reviews progress	9/15	22/34	34/21	32/30	3/0	10.20*
3	Lets you know what's expected	13/20	37/46	20/22	27/12	3/0	11.33*
4	Delegates sufficient authority	28/45	42/37	16/15	7/3	7/0	12.91*
5	Actively supports your ideas	5/16	33/40	44/39	15/4	3/1	17.09**
6	Demonstrates concern with development	12/21	27/35	27/31	21/11	13/2	14.96**
7	Coaches and guides effectively	6/15	24/36	37/42	24/7	9/0	24.90***
8	Committed to team building	22/38	33/32	28/26	13/3	4/1	12.41*
9	Encourages good relationships	21/41	36/32	30/22	9/5	4/0	13.06*
10	Creates a trusting environment	15/29	28/35	32/29	17/7	8/0	17.54**
11	Is a good listener	17/27	37/40	25/26	16/6	5/1	9.56*
12	Shows genuine interest	12/29	33/34	32/28	18/7	5/2	13.46**

Significance levels: * = 0.05, ** = 0.01, *** = 0.001

Figure 10.8 *Comparison of 1991/92 percentages using Chi-squared (1991/92 percentages based on n = 194/193)*

11 Changes in levels of effectiveness

The ultimate objective of training and development is to increase effectiveness in part of the organization. This is why the organization invests money in it. Yet many will argue that training, and in particular management training, cannot be evaluated against organizational effectiveness. This is either because the changes due to training become indistinguishable from the effects of other events or because the effort of an individual has little effect upon the performance of the organization as a whole. There is some truth in these arguments. It is difficult to isolate the effects of training from other factors and it may be impossible to do this if the criteria by which change is to be monitored have not been established before the training is designed. It is also true that the efforts of any one individual are unlikely to have a noticeable effect on the balance sheet at the end of the year.

There is, however, no need to use such a general criterion when looking for improvements in organizational effectiveness. It is possible to focus on a small part of the organization and to link improvements in its performance with training interventions. In this section we will show how this can be done. Where possible we will use actual cases to support the argument.

Individual changes in effectiveness

Most training and development activities focus on the individual, with the intention that the learning will enable him or her to become more effective either in the present job or one which is shortly to be attempted.

If the training need which is to be met is identified in terms of the improved performance which should result (rather than that 'Mr X needs to attend course Y'), then it should be possible after the programme to assess whether this improvement has taken place. This may be quantifiable as an increase in productivity. It might also be expressed as having a wider range of skills and thus offering increased flexibility of employment.

In an earlier section on using behaviour scales for assessing change (page 102), it was suggested that these could make explicit what changes were likely and that it might be possible to integrate them with annual performance appraisal categories. If this can be done, the employing managers will be able to provide evidence of whether changes have taken place and, if so, whether increased effectiveness is the result. The study by Latham and Saari (1979) was referred to (page 58) when we were discussing behaviour modelling as a training method. One of the methods of assessing increased performance in this study was an improvement in ratings on the annual appraisal. It was also possible to show increased productivity in the sections for which the supervisors were responsible.

There is a difference between having relevant skills and using them in appropriate situations to achieve high levels of performance. One of the key variables here is 'self-efficacy'; the perception of how able one is to successfully carry through a course of action required to deal with a particular situation (Bandura 1977, 1986). High self-efficacy may thus be a formal objective of training. For instance, Donnison (1993) measured self-efficacy of first line managers before and after a programme of outdoor management development. A list of the 30 most important aspects of the job (in a particular financial sector organization) was generated from critical incident and rep-grid interviews. Items like the following emerged from this process:

- managing your own time
- motivating and encouraging staff to achieve goals
- leading staff by setting standards
- communicating information to and from staff
- monitoring the performance of staff
- maintaining standards and quality of work
- allocating and controlling available resources
- making decisions.

Some 90 first line managers were asked to rate their self-efficacy on each of the 30 items, using a 10-point scale (1 = not confident to 10 = completely confident) before and after the programme. Most of the first line managers had higher self-efficacy scores after the programme and the changes were particularly noticeable in those who had low self-efficacy scores before the programme.

The level of post-training self-efficacy may be important in itself, but it is also likely to be a predictor of long-term transfer and persistence in trying to do something despite an unsupportive work situation (Marx, 1982). Another variable which is associated with effectiveness in the work situation is goal setting. There is a great deal of evidence that individuals who set specific and difficult goals are likely to exert more effort and perform at a higher level than those who set general ('do your best') and less difficult goals (Locke and Latham, 1990).

Goal setting is also regarded by many as an important factor in the transfer of learning (Baldwin and Ford, 1988). Thus one way of facilitating the transfer of learning back to work is by the use of action planning during the training. At intervals during the training the participants are asked to focus on the utility of what has been discussed. This can be done by giving out coloured sheets of paper and asking each participant to write down things which have been covered during the day that are thought likely to be particularly useful back at work. They should also make a short note against each on how they intend to make use of it. Some sharing and discussing of these will give useful feedback on what they think is important learning, but the main purpose is to focus on utility and build up an action plan for when they return to work. Towards the end of the programme they cluster the items from the sheets into areas and then arrange them in some order of priority. The action plan for (say) the next six months is now drafted by putting some time frame on each area to be tackled. It will also be necessary to write down against each area likely countervailing forces and how these are to be overcome. The questions which need to be addressed will include the following:

- Will this action have an effect on other people? How will they react to it?
- Whose authority will be necessary to implement this action? How do I ensure that this will be available?
- What organizational constraints are likely to prevent this action? What can be done to ease them?

The action plan is a piece of positive management. It forms a set of goals to be achieved and gives a time frame and rationale for each of them. It can be lodged with the course tutors and followed up later. Whether this happens or not, the plan should be discussed with the employing manager, before or after return to work. During the follow-up some six months later, questions like the following can be asked:

- How much of your action plan have you been able to implement?
- Which actions have been shelved and why?
- What positive benefits in terms of effectiveness in your part of the organization have resulted from carrying out your action plan?

Subject experts set goals which are very different from those of beginners; they are usually more specific, more difficult, more hierarchical and have within them clearer statements of how contingencies are to be managed (Locke and Latham, 1990). If training is to be considered as a process for turning beginners into experts, an assessment of the quality of the action plans along these dimensions may be a useful form of evaluation of progress.

A specific form of action planning is through the use of an organizational project as the focus for the learning, with input from tutors at stages throughout the project. This project often has as a focus the increased effectiveness of a part of the company, and can show a good return for the investment in training. An example of this was described by Woodward (1975). The programme investigated was for supervisors and led to a National Examinations Board in Supervisory Studies qualification. There was formal course work, mainly on theories of management, which was examined. There was also a work-based project, which was intended to show the advantages of good supervisory practice.

Woodward was unable to show any differences in ways of working as a result of the theoretical part of the course. This ought not to surprise us. We have considered good examples of the processes which are needed in order to change the ways in which people do things at work. Theoretical input on the nature of management, without role play or work-based practice, is not one of them. Woodward was able to estimate the benefits of the project work, and 6 of the 12 showed positive benefits. Averaged over the 12, the return on training investment (course fee, travel, subsistence, equipment costs, pay of trainees and covering costs) was 2.9 : 1.

In the Department of Organizational Psychology at Birkbeck College, University of London, we have been encouraging our PhD students to form into groups (cohorts) in order to participate in mutual exchange of ideas, experience and learning (action learning sets). For example, a topic in which one of the lecturers is interested (e.g. stress at work, organizational change in the public sector, evaluation of training) is selected as the theme. A cohort of four to six students who are interested in the topic is selected from applicants and each carries out his or her own work-based research. The main theme of the research is negotiated with the organization to which the student belongs and a senior manager takes responsibility for facilitating access. The group meets at least once a month to discuss plans and progress. Most of the meetings are devoted to discussing, in some depth, issues raised by one of the cohort. The main focus here is to develop the ability of each student to carry out research and thus to reach Doctoral standard. The process is more successful than the more normal one of individually based PhD programmes (which are also run concurrently), probably because it offers a good deal of support and encouragement to part-time students who otherwise become quite isolated for long periods. There is also the motivational aspect of goal setting, as within this process is the necessity to have reached certain (self-set) stages before reporting progress to the next meeting. The work-based projects are often valuable to the organization and show a good return on investment (academic fees for three years plus some two dozen days away from work discussing work-related issues).

Changes in the effectiveness of teams

Introduction

Team development is intended to improve the effectiveness of a group of people whose jobs require that they work together. It assumes:

- that the group has some reason for existing, some common goals and problems
- that interdependent action is required to achieve the goals or solve the problems
- that it is valuable to spend time in trying to understand and improve the way in which group members work together to achieve their tasks.

Team development activities may focus on working relationships or on action planning. There are three main models: problem solving, interpersonal, and role-identification.

- The *problem-solving* model encourages the group to identify problem areas which are affecting the achievement of group goals. Action planning is then used as a method of tackling the problems.
- The *interpersonal* model attempts to improve decision making and problem solving by increasing communication and cooperation on the assumption that improving interpersonal skills increases the effectiveness of the team.
- The *role-identification* model attempts to increase effectiveness by increasing understanding of the interacting roles within the group.

It is, of course, possible to combine the different models. For instance, the Blake and Mouton (1964) Managerial Grid is a combination of problem-solving and interpersonal approaches. For simplicity we will select a well-known example of each of the three models separately and examine the problems of trying to use them to improve the effectiveness of teams.

Problem-solving groups

The most widely used example of the problem-solving model is found in 'quality circles'. A quality circle is a small group of people involved in similar working situations who meet to discuss work-related problems. They usually volunteer to do this, i.e. it is not part of their job description.

Implicit in the definition of a quality circle is that it is sanctioned by the organization and meets in the firm's time. The group:

- brainstorms problems
- agrees priorities
- selects and defines the problems to be tackled
- works together to collect data, etc.

- agrees possible solutions to problems
- presents proposals to management.

The group has a leader, who may be the supervisor, but the group sometimes elects its own leader from among the members. At least in the early stages, the group will also have a facilitator who helps with process issues. There is a very large literature on quality circles; a useful review of it may be found in van Fleet and Griffin (1989).

In order for quality circles to flourish, Ishikawa (1968) has identified eight main principles:

1 All levels of senior management must agree to support, encourage and listen to circle activities.
2 Management must not use circles to further their own pet ideas. Circles must be free to pursue their own priorities.
3 Management must be patient—circles do not produce change overnight.
4 Managers must be prepared to accept failures without recrimination but with encouragement.
5 Participation must be present in every step of the process.
6 Circle leaders and facilitators must be carefully chosen, well trained and credible.
7 Facilitators must be given enough time and support for them to carry out their activities of improving group processes.
8 Circle membership must be voluntary.

The Ishikawa principles, which are extracted from the Japanese experience, predict with remarkable accuracy the failures of quality circles programmes in the UK and the USA. Violation of one or more of these principles usually leads to the failure of the quality circle.

Dale and Ball (1983) carried out a survey of 86 companies in the UK which were supporting more than 1000 quality circles. For our purpose, the main interest is in criteria of success.

Some 92 per cent of the companies claimed that their quality circles programme was successful. The main reasons given for this were thorough consultation at all levels in the company and full management commitment to the concept. Also thought to be important was a controlled and gradual development without expectation of immediate cost savings. Thorough training and the selection of an enthusiastic facilitator were also considered to be essential.

Members of the circles found that there were benefits. Increased job satisfaction, better teamwork within the department, recognition of their achievements and better relationships with members of management were quoted.

There were also benefits to management, and the three considered most important were that first line supervisors were placed in a leadership role; that many problems were solved at grass roots level, thus allowing management to concentrate on higher priority items; and that it was possible to identify future managers among the quality circle membership.

Overall, the companies felt that the main benefits derived from the investment in quality circles were:

- increased involvement of employees
- improvement in quality and productivity
- a reduction of the barriers between management and shopfloor
- improvement in communications across the company.

Dale and Ball conclude that quality circles may lead to significant cost savings, but in some organizations they will do no more than make minor improvements. However, quality circles often improve the quality of working life, and this is a worthwhile gain.

There is, of course, the other side of the coin—some quality circle projects fail. Dale and Hayward (1984) discuss some of the reasons for these failures. Most of these, as was stated above, could be attributed to disregarding one or more of the principles extracted by Ishikawa.

Working on interpersonal skills

Where team development is undertaken using an interpersonal model, the intention is to increase communication, sharing, trust, collaboration and cohesiveness within the group. This was, of course, the intention of the T-Groups which were so popular in some American organizations in the 1960s. The T-Group has had a bad press in the evaluation literature, usually because individuals were *required* to attend and deeply resented the intrusion to their privacy which was involved. More recent forms of team development are rather less intrusive and there is less coercion to attend.

In an extensive and critical review of the role of team development in organizational effectiveness, Woodman and Sherwood (1980) report that team development based upon interpersonal skills is often used as an aid to the formation of a new team, but their main conclusion was that the available research does not provide a reliable link between this kind of team building and improved work group performance. A more recent review of the research on team building, by Tannenbaum *et al* (1992), also supports this view. However, they indicate that team development activities, based upon interpersonal skills development, are likely to have some effect on attitudes—how one feels about others, the workplace, the value of the team, satisfaction with the work. Many would argue that improvements in indices of these attitudes would be valuable in themselves as indicators of well-being at work. It is also possible that such improvements will be negatively associated with measures of stress, levels of sickness, absenteeism and turnover.

Identification of roles   The role-identification model approach treats the group as a set of interacting roles and attempts to increase effectiveness by a better understanding and allocation of these roles. Each member of a team is considered to contribute in two ways: (1) in a functional role, drawing on professional and technical knowledge; and (2) in a team role, helping the progress of the team towards achieving its objectives. This implies that a team can only deploy its technical resources to best advantage when team members recognize and use their team strengths. Observation of groups where three or four people who are outstanding in their field are recruited to form a team indicates that the team performs in a disappointing way—usually everyone produces ideas and no-one develops them.

One of the best known team role approaches is that advocated by Belbin (1981). Belbin's theory is based upon research using management games where team effectiveness was measured in terms of 'financial' results. This is an interesting training and evaluation procedure—to form teams through a role analysis and then test their performance in the controlled situation produced by a management game. There is, however, a question concerning the validity of this as there is not much evidence so far that the identification of roles results in increased performance in job settings.

The model may well have some value in setting up project teams where roles can be allocated and the strengths of others (apart from their technical ability) need to be understood. However, it probably has greater value in providing a vehicle for helping the group members to conceptualize the roles necessary and for developing their skills in roles which they had not previously considered. It ought to be possible to evaluate on a pre-/post-basis how people's perceptions of their roles have changed and the extent to which they perceive the group as being more effective as a result of the training. Such information has not yet been published.

Evaluation of team-based strategies   Not much of the published research on various strategies for team building permits unambiguous interpretation of the results (Woodman and Sherwood, 1980; Tannenbaum *et al*, 1992). The main problem is one of internal validity, i.e. the confidence with which conclusions can be drawn from a set of data. The research designs are usually poor, and it is not possible to rule out alternative explanations for the effects which are reported (i.e. low internal validity).

The problem-solving approach is easier to evaluate than the others, as the problems to be tackled are clearly identified and defined and they often have an obvious connection with some measure of organizational effectiveness. It can often be argued that the increase in effectiveness would not have occurred without the development of the team. It may also be possible to calculate the value to the organization of solving a particular problem. This might be done directly or by estimating how much consultant time has been saved.

The interpersonal approach is usually evaluated in terms of perceived effectiveness. This is not very convincing if the intervention needs to be justified in terms of organizational benefit, as the results are likely to be measured as changes in attitude rather than in behaviour. There is also the problem of internal validity as, without the use of control groups, it may be difficult to rule out factors other than the team development process which could have affected the attitudes measured. Causal links are very difficult to establish because of the interaction between the things being measured. For instance, one of my students attempted to link members' satisfaction with team performance. He was carrying out some team development activities within a company offering financial services and wanted to check satisfaction with team processes, etc. He developed a measure and, when testing this, found that team scores correlated positively with performance (measured in terms of volume of business done in the last month). Does this mean that satisfaction leads to higher performance? If greater satisfaction does lead to better performance, measures of satisfaction taken now should predict performance during the coming months. This was tested, but the correlation was negligible. The implication of this is that it is more likely that higher performance leads to greater satisfaction than vice versa. This is not an isolated finding. Mullen and Cooper (1994) report a meta-analysis of studies which examined the relationship between cohesiveness and effectiveness. They found a positive relationship, but concluded that the direction of causality was *from* rather than *to* performance. Teams which perform well tend to become more cohesive.

Evaluation is even more difficult with the use of the role clarification approach in an organizational setting. The composition of each group is unique and the assessment of its improved effectiveness will therefore have the format of a case study. It should be possible to analyse a set of these to indicate perceived improvements in group working which support the theory. These perceived improvements will certainly imply increased awareness on the part of the group members, but the links with improved effectiveness of the organization are not easy to predict.

Changes in organizational effectiveness

Introduction Organizational effectiveness is not a simple concept with only the balance sheet at the end of the year as the criterion to be assessed. There are many ways in which one can look at it, and many writers have offered sets of criteria. One of the early attempts was that of Georgeopolous and Tannenbaum (1957), who evaluated effectiveness in terms of productivity, flexibility and the absence of organizational strain. More familiar is the approach of Blake and Mouton (1964), which seeks the simultaneous achievement of high production-centred and high people-centred methods of management. Katz and Kahn (1978) argue for growth, survival and control over the environment.

A more recent classification has been offered by Cameron (1980), who considers that almost all views on organizational effectiveness can be summarized under four headings:

1 *Goal-directed* definitions focus on the output of the organization, how close it comes to meeting its goals.
2 *Resource-acquiring* definitions judge effectiveness by the extent to which the organization acquires needed resources from its external environment.
3 *Constituencies* are groups of individuals who have some stake in the organization—resource providers, customers, etc.—and effectiveness is judged in terms of how well the organization responds to the demands and expectations of these groups.
4 *Internal process* definitions focus the attention on flows of information, absence of strain and levels of trust as measures of effectiveness.

I have found this classification of Cameron's to be very useful when discussing evaluation of training events with line managers. It is possible to consider effectiveness at levels lower than that of the whole organization and thus to build up a matrix like that in Figure 11.1.

	Individual (my work)	Work Group (my section)	Function (my dept)	Regional level	Organizational level
Goal-directed					
Resource-acquiring					
Satisfying constituencies					
Internal processes					

Figure 11.1 *The organizational effectiveness matrix*

The matrix can be used to discuss desirable changes in effectiveness which might accrue from training or development events. These should be identified by type of effectiveness and the level at which they will be measured. It is important first of all to establish what criteria the line managers are actually using to assess effectiveness and by what criteria they themselves are being judged. The next stage is to identify the risks and related costs if these criteria are not achieved. A good deal of this can come from critical incident interviews based on unusual occurrences which caused a disruption of work or a failure to achieve the levels expected. The classification suggested by Cameron is a useful one for content analysis of these interviews. In order to explain how this might be done, we need a more detailed description of the types.

Goal-directed   The most widely used approach to effectiveness focuses on meeting goals and targets. Directing and sustaining goal-directed effort by employees is a continuous task for most managers, but assessments will usually be a series of point measures over time. Most organizations use basic measurement of work output to meet *product* goals, where the emphasis is on quality or quantity, variety uniqueness or innovativeness of whatever is being produced. Types of indices which are usually available are:

Quantity	Quality	Variety
units produced	defects/failure rate	diversity of product range
tasks completed	reject rates	rationalization of product range
applications, etc. processed	error rates	new product/service innovation
backlogs	rework	
turnover	scrap	
units sold	waste	
money collected	shortages	
on-time deliveries	accidents	

An example of increasing effectiveness, where this was defined as meeting goals, was provided by NORWEB.

In January 1990, three months before the privatization of the electricity supplier NORWEB, an analysis of the organization's performance showed that the Peak Area trailed behind other parts of the region. It had high revenue costs, high overtime levels and was not meeting NORWEB's guaranteed standards of service.

Workshops were introduced in which managers were encouraged to use a more consultative management style. Each manager left the workshop with an agreed individual development plan. Team development workshops for first line managers and their teams were also introduced.

One year later, revenue costs showed a saving of £960 000, overtime savings of £500 000 were made and the Peak Area had achieved all of its guaranteed standards of service. All sickness rate targets were also beaten and this showed a saving of £100 000 on the year.

Source: National Training Awards, 1992

There are also *system* goals, which emphasize growth, profits, modes of functioning, return on investment, etc. Criteria which might be available are:

productivity	rates of achieving deadlines	work stoppages
processing time	output per person/ hour	supervisory time
profit	on-time shipments	amount of overtime
operating costs	percentage of quota achieved	lost time
running costs	percentage of tasks incorrectly done	machine down-time
performance/ cost ratio	efficiency	frequency of accidents
variability of product or service		
length of time to train new employees	accident costs	
time to bring in new products and services		

Increases in manpower, facilities, assets, sales, etc., compared with own past state and with competitors.

In 1991 Hoover faced significant difficulties because of overcapacity in the supply of white goods in the European Community. Investigation into company processes revealed a lack of efficiency and flexibility.

The workforce was trained in 'just-in-time' philosophy and methods and individuals were encouraged to have a greater sense of involvement in the running of their work areas.

Productivity (output per person) increased by 93 per cent, scrap was reduced by 50 per cent and inventory reduced from £10.1 million to £2.5 million. Manufacturing lead time was reduced from six weeks to one week.

Source: National Training Awards, 1992

'Just-in-time' methods are good examples of improving the effectiveness of systems within the organization and they are usually monitored by the setting of system goals.

Most of the techniques which are used for monitoring the achievement of system goals are fragmentary because they focus on a specific part of the company. Some method of looking at the workflow through the organization, perhaps like that described by Chapple and Sayles (1961), can overcome this problem and offer criteria by which system goals can be assessed at the level of the whole organization.

Acquiring resources

Looking at resources changes the emphasis from outputs, goals and targets, to inputs designed to achieve some competitive advantage. At the level of the organization, the evaluation might be a comparison with major competitors or against 'how we did last year' or against some ideal desired state. At lower levels, increased flexibility is often the measure which is used. Criteria which might be available for assessing increases in effectiveness include:

increases in number of customers	increase in the pool of trained staff
new branches opened	skills for future job requirements developed
new markets entered	increased flexibility in job deployment developed
takeover of other organizations	readiness to perform some task if asked to do so
ability to change standard operating procedures when necessary	flexibility in meeting changing customer requirements

---

Prospect Foods, a catering-to-retailing family business, found that it was difficult to recruit well-motivated young people during 1989. A survey revealed a good deal of public prejudice against many of the key skills involved in producing and serving food.

Links were set up with local schools, i.e. headteachers and career guidance teachers spent some time on attachment to the company, and pupils took part in two-week industrial placements. Employees from Prospect Foods also went into schools to work on a range of projects.

In the following year, the number of young recruits doubled and their quality improved. During the same period, net profits for the company increased by almost a half and a series of catering awards were won by the company's tea shops.

Source: **National Training Awards, 1991**

From our perspective, the example is one of increased effectiveness by ensuring necessary resources, good quality recruits.

Devolving accountability and responsibility to departments is widely seen as contributing to the flexibility of organizations faced with an ever-changing environment. Training is a necessary part of this process and can be evaluated on the basis of what effects would have been likely if no training had been offered.

> **In 1992 Ladbroke Racing decided to abolish the existing system of using peripatetic relief managers to relieve absent betting shop managers. Instead, the betting shop staff were trained on-the-job to become multi-skilled so that any absences could be covered within the existing shop team. The intention was to enable the employees to be more flexible and thus to increase the value of the human resources available.**
>
> **There has been a significant reduction in labour turnover and an increase in commitment to the shop team. The total attributable saving by the end of 1994, when the phasing out of the relief manager grade will be completed, has been estimated at £3.5 million.**
>
> *Source*: **National Training Awards, 1993**

Constituencies Effectiveness can be judged by the extent to which the organization meets the expectations of groups whose cooperation is important. Assessment of effectiveness will be against criteria like the following:

customer complaints	company image surveys
returned material	customer relations surveys
repair orders on guarantee	recall costs
non-receipt of goods	incorrect goods received
product or service quality	meeting statutory requirements
awareness of customer problems	on-time deliveries

Most organizations monitor criteria of this nature, but few publish the information. One rather useful study which attempted to relate this kind of criterion with training was that by Massey (1957). He described a programme of Post Office training and showed that the number of misdeliveries and errors (as well as absence without reporting and abuse of sick leave) decreased in the trained group when compared with an 'untrained' group.

Customer satisfaction is a criterion which many organizations take seriously. For instance, in 1990 Pavilion Services (operating 11 motorway service stations throughout England and Wales) undertook market research which revealed a low level of satisfaction among its customers. The key to the problem appeared to be the ineffectiveness of the shift supervisors. A total of some 110 of these supervisors were trained off-the-job on modules like task management, leadership and motivation and staff rights and responsibilities. Market research in 1992 showed that Pavilion Services had risen to the top of the list of service areas in customer satisfaction (National Training Awards, 1992).

The word 'constituents' can also be used to describe groups within the organization as these are, of course, interdependent in some ways. Assessment of satisfaction will then mean asking the question, 'How do others value what we do?' Ford Europe used this procedure in an organizational development programme. In 1981, faced with a major threat from Japanese manufacturers, Ford decided to improve the effectiveness of their European operation. The top 200 managers were brought together for a few days and were grouped by function—production, marketing, personnel, etc. They were asked to comment on how the other functions helped or hindered their work. Thus the senior production managers worked in a room writing on flipcharts what it was that another function (say, personnel) did that was helpful to them and what they did that hindered them. This was repeated for all the other functions. The other functions also wrote up their opinions. The second phase of the workshop was to reorganize the paper so that each function had a room which was papered with the views of others about them. For instance, the personnel managers would go back to their room to find all the positive remarks from all the other functions on one of their walls and all the negative ones on another wall (or two!). A good deal of the information generated had not previously been available and it was found to be useful. The managers started to think about ways in which the functions could make greater contributions to organizational effectiveness. The workshop then proceeded with some facilitation of intergroup processes which led to a greater commitment to working with other groups to improve the effectiveness of the organization (rather than just that of the parent function).

This is a good example of increasing effectiveness, defined as the extent to which the organization meets the expectations of groups whose cooperation is important.

Internal processes Under this heading, effective organizations are defined as those in which there is little internal strain, little intergroup conflict, where members feel integrated with the system and where information flows smoothly. Assessment of effectiveness may be against hard data like turnover of employees, absence, sick leave, etc., but it is often also against surveyed opinions of 'how we were' or 'how we would like to be'. The feeling of belonging and commitment often predisposes people to put in extra effort to achieve organizational goals. At the group level, this used to be called morale. Although the word now sounds old-fashioned, the concept is still important. It can sometimes be assessed by measuring such things as:

- whether people are aware of the organization's vision, strategy and plans
- whether the staff believe that effort will be rewarded
- the motivating climate
- job involvement
- job satisfaction
- group cohesiveness
- commitment
- upstream planning, i.e. anticipating what might go wrong and preventing that from happening.

Measures of these kinds of attitudes were the main interest of the organizational development movement which was so powerful in the USA during the 1970s, and many survey instruments have been developed by consultants and researchers. Useful sources of these inventories are the books by Henerson *et al* (1978), Cook *et al* (1981) and Seashore *et al* (1982).

Poor morale may show in the statistics of:

transfer/turnover	disciplinary actions
absenteeism	grievances
medical visits	stoppages
accident rates	excessive work breakdown

If they are prevalent, such things can be very expensive. Mirvis and Macy (1982) estimate the cost of one day's absence at US$80.06, that of turnover of an employee at US$160.65 and that of a grievance at US$54.52 (all at 1976 values).

In 1989, Lucas Aerospace were faced with a serious graduate turnover problem as, typically, the company would lose 30 per cent of new graduate recruits within the first year. A new process of induction training was introduced for the 58 graduates in the 1990 intake. Only one of the group left the company during the first year (as opposed to the 17 which would have been predicted from the old rate). The saving for the company was estimated at almost a quarter of a million pounds (National Training Awards, 1991).

Another example was provided by Dollond and Aitchison, the ophthalmic and optical dispensing group, who found that they had an unacceptable rate of 60 per cent annual turnover of receptionists. These employees felt that they had few skills and little scope for advancement.

As a result, they showed little job satisfaction. All of the receptionists were trained in clinical and dispensing skills and were regraded as optical assistants. Turnover reduced from 60 to 21 per cent, the recruitment costs saved paid for the training and the average sales per optical assistant increased by 13 per cent (National Training Awards, 1993).

Training can have a marked impact upon the patterns of work within parts of the organization, for instance, by increasing the quality of decision making, of planning or of supervision. Training can help to improve working within groups and between groups. It can also help people to cope with reduced staff levels and with managing time better. Many of these activities can affect the attitudes of managers and staff, and these changes may affect the statistics associated with low morale.

I hope that this rather detailed description and these examples have given you something of the flavour of the four categories of effectiveness. I suggest that you try to use the matrix shown in Figure 11.1 by mapping onto it the changes in effectiveness which you might expect from a particular programme. These can be at the level of the individual, the group or one of the higher levels (the higher the better). The changes might be expected in more than one category of effectiveness. I have found this exercise to be useful when discussing with line managers exactly what is supposed to change as a result of a training programme and how this change is to be measured. This, as you will remember, was thought likely to be one of the problems in trying to use the training model which is shown in Figure 4.3 (page 38).

It is interesting, as a theoretical exercise, to attempt some mapping of possible changes for courses which are already running. You might try it for yourselves with a programme which is designed for individuals at a certain level in the organization—say, principles of management for junior managers, and then again with a programme which is 'tailor-made' for improving the effectiveness of a particular individual or group at work. What criteria can you measure? Which kind of programme do you find easier to evaluate?

Another very useful method for identifying criteria of organizational effectiveness is offered by the European model for Total Quality Management. Effectiveness is defined in terms of nine elements:

- the *enablers*: leadership, policy and strategy, people management, resources and processes
- the *results*: customer satisfaction, people satisfaction, impact on society and business results.

The EFQM recommends a method of self-appraisal of parts of the organization against each of these nine elements:

Leadership is defined as 'the behaviour of all managers in driving the organization towards total quality'. Assessors would be looking for:

- visible involvement of managers as role models, being accessible and communicating
- recognition of the efforts and successes of individuals and teams
- provision of appropriate resources and assistance
- involvement with 'customers' and 'suppliers' both inside and outside the organization.

Policy and strategy should be assessed by how:

- TQM is reflected in mission and strategy statements
- policy and strategy are affected by feedback from customers and suppliers, from staff, from benchmarking against competitors
- policy and strategy are communicated
- policy and strategy are regularly reviewed and improved.

People management should be assessed by how:

- continuous improvement of people management is achieved by planning, communicating and using the perceptions of staff
- the skills pool is maintained and developed
- performance management is carried out
- staff are involved in continuous improvement.

Resources should be optimized, and areas for assessment should include:

- the management of financial resources
- the management of material resources
- the use of technology
- the availability and the use made of information.

Processes which are important are identified and reviewed to ensure continuous improvement. Assessment will focus on how:

- critical processes are defined and identified
- impact on the business is evaluated
- the organization manages its processes
- performance measures are used to review processes and set targets for improvement.

Customer satisfaction, i.e. what the perception of customers (direct and indirect) is of the company and its products and services. This should be monitored regularly as it is central to the survival of any organization.

People satisfaction. The intention here is to satisfy the needs and expectations of all staff by good human relations policies and activities—awareness, involvement, development, reward, job security, health and safety.

Impact on society implies that a total quality approach should satisfy the needs and expectations of the community at large. Areas to be assessed should include:

- active involvement in the community
- activities to reduce and prevent nuisance and harm to neighbours
- indirect measures of impact on society, complaints, incidents, etc.

Business results are defined as 'what the organization is achieving in relation to its planned performance'. Areas could include:

- financial targets
- targets and objectives for processes and systems
- targets for products, services or market share.

There is a good deal of detail in the descriptions of the elements of the model and in the assessment pack (EFQM, 1993). From our point of view, as evaluators, the model is helpful because it helps to identify the main operations and establishes objectives for improvement which are based upon criteria of organizational effectiveness. The EFQM model has the advantage over the Cameron (1980) categories, which were described earlier, in that it allows detailed examination of 'enablers' as well as 'results'. It thus offers a much more complex model of organizational effectiveness and is therefore more valuable to us in our search for criteria against which to evaluate.

Returning to the subject of the second part of this book, training as an effective process, I would argue that something like this EFQM model or the matrix developed from Cameron's work should be used to focus attention on areas of effectiveness. Before the programme is designed, decisions should be made about where the changes in effectiveness are expected to occur and how they should be measured. Before an individual or group is accepted for training, the indices of effectiveness which will change as a result of training should be established.

12 Costing changes

This section on evaluating changes would not be complete without some mention of costing, cost-effectiveness and cost benefit analysis. Although few trainers carry out detailed costing activities, some flavour of what is involved in relating costs to results is useful in thinking through the logic of an evaluation. Some of the words which we have been using have rather different definitions when applied to costs and benefits, and it is worth while stating these to set the scene:

- Improving efficiency means achieving the same results with lower costs.
- Improving effectiveness means achieving better results with the same costs.
- It is possible to get better results with lower costs, and this is called improved productivity.

Costing

Costing systems vary from one organization to another, and liaison with the accounting department is usually necessary to make sure that the system adopted for training costs is compatible with other costing systems within the organization. A simple matrix for costing training events is shown in Figure 12.1.

	Personnel	Facilities	Equipment
Design	1a	1b	1c
Delivery	2a	2b	2c
Evaluation	3a	3b	3c

Figure 12.1   Costing training events

Design

The cost of design can be spread over the life of the programme (i.e. shared by the proposed number of programmes) as it will otherwise account for some 50 per cent of the overall costs. As a rough guideline, technical courses will need some five hours preparation per hour of delivery. Programmed or packaged instruction will be much more expensive, as up to 100 hours of design are needed for one hour of instruction. With computer-based learning, the ratio can be as high as 400 : 1. The cost of designing the learning event will include things like:

1(a) Costs of preliminary analysis of training needs, development of objectives, course development, lesson planning, programming, audio-visual aids production, consultant advice, contractors.

1(b) Offices, telephones.

1(c) Production of workbooks, slides, tapes, tests, programmes, printing and reproduction.

Delivery The cost of actually running the event will include:

2(a) Some proportion of annual salaries of trainers, lecturers, trainees, clerical/administration staff; costs of consultants and outside lecturers; travel costs.

2(b) Cost of conference centres or upkeep of classrooms, buildings, offices; accommodation and food; office supplies and expenses.

2(c) Equipment for delivering the training—slide projectors, videos, computers, simulators, workbooks, maintenance and repair of aids; expendable training materials or some proportion of cost relative to lifetime; handouts; hire of films, videos, etc.

Evaluation The cost of evaluation is usually low compared to the other two elements. Probable costs include:

3(a) Cost of designing questionnaires, etc., follow-up interviews, travel, accommodation; analysis and summary of data collected; delivering the evaluation report.

3(b) Offices, telephones.

3(c) Tests, questionnaires, postage.

To give a complete picture, it is also worth considering a general overhead for the expense of maintaining the training department. This may be allocated to individual training programmes on the basis of hours of participant learning, tutor involvement and level of administration required.

Salaries of trainees are often not allocated to training costs on the basis that a certain amount of 'slack' is necessary for effectiveness. For instance, when a foreman is taken off the factory floor for a few hours a week to discuss supervisory methods, it makes very little difference to his 'output' as a foreman. In such a case it seems wrong to include the value of his salary for the hours spent as a cost to training. However, in the survey reported by Weinstein and Kasl (1982), the salary of trainees averaged about a third of all training costs. If this is the case for a programme which is being planned, then it seems worth while to account for it and use it as a criterion when deciding training priorities.

Cost-effectiveness comparisons

Cost-effectiveness analysis allows us to cost programmes and use this as a basis for comparing them. Usually an assumption is made that the level of effectiveness of the programmes will be similar and thus the cheaper, more efficient, form of delivery would be chosen. It is, of course, also possible to compare the effectiveness of the programmes and then offer a rationale for deciding whether the increased effectiveness of one programme justifies the extra cost. This comparison is more convincing when pilot versions of the two programmes can be run, so that actual, rather than estimated, levels of effectiveness can be used. An example might help your understanding of what is involved.

One of the High Street clearing banks was interested to compare the use of computer-based learning (CBL) with delivering a traditional five-day off-job programme. The course was designed to teach some aspects of bank work connected with lending money on mortgages. It was a knowledge-based programme, and some of it was at the 'analytic' level, i.e. analysing a situation so that the correct procedure can be selected (see page 73). The CBL package was produced and, in piloting, it was found that the average trainee could complete it in three days. It was intended that the three days would be spent in the branch at which the trainee worked or one very close to it and that the learning should be spaced at regular intervals during slack periods.

Costings were made for the development, delivery and evaluation of the CBL method. The delivery aspect was rather provisional as it was not known just how much coordination would be necessary for it to work well. (One of the problems with open learning systems is to achieve the amount of structure which is necessary to allow the trainees to develop their learning in a systematic way. An hour or so here and there does not produce optimum learning.) The traditional five-day course had been running for some time and could be costed accurately. The development costs were spread over the number of people likely to be trained in three years. It was thus possible to make a comparison on the basis of estimated cost per student trained on each of the systems.

The systems could also be compared on an estimate of effectiveness:

- Shorter training time and less time away from work on the CBL system
- Less travel time and expense for the CBL users
- Less covering costs for trainees on the CBL package
- Better learning gain on the CBL package
- Some increment in computer literacy among staff using the CBL.

A further basis for comparison of effectiveness would be the preference of the trainees for the methods being offered. Some would no doubt like to get away from the workplace for five days. Some would like to learn with others. There may also be some benefit in their discussing how work is organized differently in different branches.

In these days of 'rightsizing' and 'outsourcing', one other comparison is worth considering. What are the cost-effectiveness implications of buying in training consultants to run short courses?

Suppose that the cost of a full-time trainer is £25,000 salary, plus £10,000 a year for overheads. Such a person could deliver some 35 five-day courses/workshops a year and also have time for needs identification, preparation and holiday. The cost of delivery of a five-day programme for (say) ten participants with two trainers would thus be £2,000 plus overheads of cost of training rooms, etc.

Training consultants will provide training at rates which vary between £400 for one and £1,500 for more than one trainer per day (plus VAT). Taking a rate of £800 for two, the cost of a five-day workshop would be £4,000 (again, plus rooms, etc.).

The cost of sending 10 participants on open courses run by an agency would be some £500 per day per delegate, i.e. £25,000.

The costs can easily be compared, but there are other questions about effectiveness which might include the following:

1 Can sufficient participants be provided to justify two trainers for 35 weeks?
2 Can the trainers cover enough topics to offer 35 really useful weeks per year?
3 How does 17 weeks, with different consultants, compare with 35 weeks with two internal trainers (range of topics, expertise, numbers of delegates)?
4 If external consultants are to provide the training, who will do the needs analysis with the line managers?
5 Which method of delivery is likely to provide the most *effective* training?

Cost benefit analysis

In cost benefit analysis the intention is to discover whether the benefits from training are more valuable to the organization than the cost of the training. Whenever possible, benefits are translated into monetary terms. Many products of training can be costed:

● Product benefits, like increased volume or quality of product
● System benefits, like increased productivity or efficiency, reduced job induction training time
● 'Hygiene' benefits, like reduced turnover, absenteeism, strikes, etc.
● Reduction in accidents (perhaps costs which are inherent in not training).

The basic process is to decide what the benefits of the training are likely to be before it is carried out. The process starts with a request from a line manager for training which is intended to improve the effectiveness of some of his or her staff. The behaviours expected to change as a result of the training are agreed between the trainer responsible and the line manager, and then the benefit analysis is carried out with a group of interested parties. The composition of this group will vary, but could include supervisors/line managers, some of the proposed trainees, colleagues, staff and 'customers' (i.e. those who receive goods or services from the proposed trainees). The expected behaviours are described to each interested party and they are all asked to list likely benefits to themselves from these. Sometimes this is done in a group workshop and the procedure is very similar to the impact analysis described below; more frequently it will be done as a series of interviews. An example of what might result from such a procedure is shown in Figure 12.2.

List of behaviours expected	List of benefits to:
	Trainees
Improved skills	(perhaps)
. . . . .	● improved job prospects
. . . . .	● higher earnings
. . . . .	● access to more interesting jobs
. . . . .	● improved job satisfaction
New skills	● etc.
. . . . .	Supervisors/line managers
. . . . .	(perhaps)
More likely to	● increased output
. . . . .	● higher value of output
. . . . .	● more flexible/innovative
. . . . .	● likely to stay longer
Less likely to	● less likely to be sick/stressed
. . . . .	● less likely to be absent
. . . . .	● less need to supervise
. . . . .	● increased safety
	● etc.
	Customers
	(perhaps)
	● better quality work
	● less need to return work
	● more 'on time' deliveries
	● etc.

Figure 12.2 *Cost benefit analysis of a proposed training event*

It is likely that some of the expected benefits can be converted into monetary returns, but, whether this is so or not, the process allows for a comparison of the likely benefits with the cost of the proposed training, and thus an informed decision of whether it is worth while to run the event. The process also establishes training objectives, defined as changes in work behaviour and increased levels of organizational effectiveness.

Impact analysis

The strength of impact analysis is that it encourages the involvement of a wide range of interested parties early in the development of the programme. The starting point is a workshop in which the 'stakeholders' discuss the objectives for the programme and the behaviours which are likely to change as a result of attending it. The word 'stakeholder' is rather more precise than the expression 'interested parties'. Stakeholders generally fall into three groups:

1 *Agents*, who produce, use or implement the programme
2 *Beneficiaries*, who profit in some way from the programme
3 *Victims*, who are negatively affected.

The next stage of the workshop is to ask each stakeholder to write down the three most important purposes of the training intervention as seen from his or her perspective. These statements are collected and pinned up on a board. The stakeholders then clarify the statements as necessary and group the purposes into clusters. Each cluster is given a title and each stakeholder is asked to allocate 10 points across the clusters. This process leads to a collective view of the main purposes of the programme and their relative importance. Having agreed on a ranking of importance the group then discuss enabling and inhibiting factors and create a force-field analysis. Finally, now that the programme has been thoroughly discussed by the interested parties, the stakeholders agree on the best ways of evaluating whether the purposes have been achieved. They may also decide that it is necessary to take benchmark measures at an early stage to allow later comparisons. The impact workshop may be reconvened, some six months after the programme has been implemented, when many of the stakeholders will have a more informed view on it and when it may be necessary to review changes to the programme.

An example of such a workshop (Bramley and Kitson, 1994) was the one which set the priorities and means of evaluating them for the suite of 14 courses on 'open systems'. These were intended to reprofile the skill base of technical staff because of the introduction of open systems and had been running for some months when the workshop took place (in September 1992). Because of the importance of these programmes, and the wide range of people who would attend, many of the functional managers were present at the workshop. The key purposes which they set for the programme, and the order of priority, are listed below:

1 To enable ICL to survive and prosper.
2 To close a skills gap and facilitate a speedy skills shift.
3 To establish a common language.
4 To create a desire for greater knowledge of the subject.
5 To improve management decision making.
6 To create a platform for better business usage of the skills.
7 To increase the extent to which people look outwards.
8 To enable individuals to innovate and influence within the company.

9 To improve the 'marketability' of individuals both internally and externally.
10 To maintain existing improvements.

The workshop participants discussed these purposes at some length and made many suggestions for impact measures. Some of these are listed below, and for each there is, in italics, a brief description of what the evaluation found (in July 1993):

1 A positive percentage shift, in particular business revenue and profit.
In 1992 and 1993 all units showed a positive movement in their revenue and profitability for 'open' products and services. ICL continues to be the only IT services supplier in the black.

2 The figure for recruitment versus rationalization costs; the resourcing of the skills internally; the potential marketability of our technical staff.
There has been a large reduction in numbers of technical staff with open systems skills who have had to be recruited from outside ICL.

3 Measure the demand for the new courses; the number of senior managers attending; the extent to which training in this area becomes a standard rather than a special offering.
Demand constantly ahead of supply. Registered interest database shows that 75 per cent converted to course places in 1993. A reasonable number of senior staff have attended more than one course.

4 The introduction of new training events in the subject.
Eleven new courses introduced during 1993 and three dropped. Five new ones to be introduced in 1994 and eight dropped. Increase in requests for local delivery of short courses on 'Open Systems'.

5 Monitor staff mobility between divisions in relation to the pre-established targets.
Staff were transferred to new divisions as planned; very few redundancies.

6 The extent to which the product portfolio includes certain products; measure customer demand for the new products.
Appropriate products were introduced as planned during 1993.

7 Sample key stakeholders and ask them to estimate which business opportunities they have been able to take advantage of directly as a result of having people trained in open systems skills.
The estimation was rather rough and ready, but came to over £10 million—this for a training investment of £0.6 million. Even if the estimates are 100 per cent out, the position is still a healthy one.

Quality awareness programmes have become very popular, and some of these lend themselves to cost/benefit studies. For instance, Girobank decided to focus on improving quality in its Operations Directorate which undertakes most of the processing and data capture functions at the main operational site. A one-day quality awareness module was developed and delivered through 69 workshops. An internal publicity campaign maintained the impetus

> of the process. There was a **22 per cent reduction in keying errors, a 28 per cent reduction in stationery reorder and a reduction in the scrutiny of customer transaction documents. The estimated saving was about £1 million from an investment of £25,000 in training.**
>
> *Source*: **National Training Awards, 1988**

Costing, cost benefit analysis and cost-effectiveness analysis are rather complex fields and we have no space to do them justice here. Interested readers are referred to Kearsley (1982), which is a useful introductory text and includes a bibliography for further reading. If you really wish to carry out such an analysis you might also look at the Cascio (1982) approach.

Value added employees

The logic underlying cost benefit analysis is not particularly appropriate to training and development activities involving managers and supervisors because the benefits are rather diffuse and take some time to be realized. A more compelling logic is to be found in considering the process as one of adding value to employees. Before training, they are considered to need extra skills, knowledge, flexibility or whatever, in order to be able to work more effectively. After training, they should be able to perform better and thus be of greater value to the organization. It should be possible to attribute some of this added value to the investment in training.

The value added approach has some assumptions underlying it, and I will attempt to make these explicit as it is described. The first assumption is to take a rather simple definition of performance at work. There is an extensive literature on why some people perform well and others do not. The complexity of the literature is increased by the inclusion of the concept of motivation; there are many theories about what encourages or discourages good performance.

For the purpose of value added accounting we need a simple theory of performance. One way in which we can achieve this is to take a simple combination of the three major elements which appear again and again in theoretical approaches. These are:

1 There is a need for some ability or *skills* in areas which are relevant to the work.
2 There must be some *motivation* to do the job (this may stem from the job context or the individual).
3 There must be the *opportunity* to use the skills and actually perform the job.

As a simple equation this can be expressed as:

Performance = Some function of (Skills × Motivation × Opportunity)

The implication of the multiplication signs is that, if there is no skill or motivation or opportunity, the performance will be zero.

This is a rather simple equation for a very complex concept. We have not attempted to state just what 'function' is involved, we have not said how we will decide which skills are relevant, nor have we attempted to operationalize 'motivation'. However, it is sometimes useful in social science to work with a 'primitive' concept which is inherently somewhat vague and imprecise, as this can make it possible to integrate seemingly disparate ideas. Certainly, with our present state of knowledge, it is not possible to produce a 'derived' concept which is precise, can be operationalized and which integrates the widely differing theories of motivation and performance which are to be found in the literature.

Value added accounting begins with a pre-training analysis which estimates the position of the individual with respect to the average level of skill and of motivation of employees who are doing that kind of work. The scaling is done against a set of proportions:

• The middle 40 per cent are considered to be about average
• Those who are *noticeably* above average will represent about 25 per cent
• Those who are *noticeably* below average will also comprise 25 per cent
• Those who are *outstandingly* good will be about 1 in 20, i.e. 5 per cent
• Those who are *outstandingly* bad will also comprise about 5 per cent.

These proportions have been deliberately chosen because they force the distribution of skills or motivation into a 'normal' statistical distribution, with the mid-points of the bands close to whole standard deviations. This is shown diagrammatically in Figure 12.3.

proportions	5%	25%	40%	25%	5%
standard deviations	−2	−1	0	+1	+2

Figure 12.3 *Normal distribution of ability*

One standard deviation (SD) above or below the mean will give a *noticeable* difference. Two SDs above or below the mean is the statistical criterion of an *outstanding* event—a significant difference.

It is possible, and for our purposes desirable, to transpose this scale of SDs into one which has 1 as its mean value. This will allow us to multiply average skills in the job by average motivation and, assuming that opportunity is available, to grade average performance as 1.

Keeping the same relative value gives centre points of the intervals .33, .67, 1, 1.33 and 1.67, i.e.:

proportions	5%	25%	40%	25%	5%
standard deviations	−2	−1	0	+1	+2
transposed scale	.33	.67	1	1.33	1.67

The transposed values are plotted on the matrix shown in Figure 12.4, which shows the effect of multiplying estimated level of skills by estimated level of motivation to give an estimated level of performance.

Estimated level of motivation	.33 Very low	.67 Below average	1.0 Average	1.33 Above average	1.67 Very high
Very high 1.67	.6	1.1	1.7	2.2	2.8
Above average 1.33	.4	.9	1.3	1.8	2.2
1.0 Average	3	.7	Average 1.0 performance	1.3	1.7
.67 Below average	.2	.4	.7	.9	1.1
.33 Very low	.1	.2	.3	.4	.6

Estimated level of skills

Figure 12.4 *Estimated levels of performance (assuming opportunity)*

Inspection of Figure 12.4 should clarify the logic of the value added approach. For instance, an employee who is considered to have average motivation (1.0) but whose skills are noticeably below average (0.67) is estimated to be performing at about 70 per cent of what is expected in the job. If training can bring such a person up to the average level of skills, the increment in performance is some 30 per cent and the value added to the employee by such training is, therefore, 30 per cent of the salary for the job.

Employees who are noticeably below average on both skills and motivation are obviously being estimated as having a very low level of performance. It may be that training is not the answer for such people and that they may be better employed in some other kind of work. Employees who are noticeably above average or who are considered to be outstanding might also be considered for redeployment. It may well be that the company could benefit from giving them a more responsible job.

Training is often aimed at improving skills or motivation. The logic of the value added approach would suggest that, if it is considered that the employees have the skills but their motivation is low, the training investment should be in supervisory and management training, with the objective of improving performance management. If the employees are thought to have the motivation but to lack some important skills, the investment should be in employee skills training.

There are some important assumptions underlying all this. Three of them need particular care:

1 Can managers allocate people to these proportions? Some managers believe that all of their people are above average. Many have great difficulty with trying to measure people on a scale of motivation.
2 Is there the opportunity to use the skills and the encouragement to maintain motivation when new skills are being used? If the opportunity is not available then the whole logic collapses.
3 Are the skills which are required for successful job performance being identified accurately, and are they those which are being learned in training?

If these assumptions can be accepted, the approach can be used to estimate the return on training investment. The estimate can also be used for forward planning of training investment. Suppose that it is intended to offer both training and group facilitation to introduce group and individual target setting which is related to the business plan. The intention would be to improve motivation by the setting of difficult targets (Locke and Latham, 1990) and increase the opportunity to use the skills available by focusing on priorities within the business plan. If this were to move most of the people, who were previously considered as average, above that norm on skills or motivation or both, the benefit to the organization would be enormous.

Cost benefit accounting, which aims to summarize all the outcomes in monetary terms, often leaves out many of the things which are important because they cannot be converted into hard cash. Value added calculations have the advantage of usually being only a part of the evaluation. The evaluation report describes the outcomes in their own terms and a conclusion is then drawn that these imply (or not) a significant increase in skills and/or motivation. The section of the report which deals with costs can then include a value added calculation which indicates that there has been some return on the investment.

Summary

Whatever the purpose of the evaluation, and no matter which approach is being used, some data collection will be necessary to answer the questions posed. What I have tried to do in this part of the book is to describe methods by which these data can be collected. In order to group the techniques for reference and for ease of explanation, I have grouped them under themes—knowledge, skills, attitudes, behaviour and effectiveness. Each of these may provide the main focus for part of an evaluation, but it should be borne in mind that learning affects the whole person and changes in levels of skills or knowledge are also likely to result in changes in confidence, self-efficacy or other attitudes.

It should also be clear that changes in effectiveness are interaction effects between levels of abilities and organizational variables. Thus, in an evaluation, we should not be satisfied with one measure of change but should look at the data from a number of different perspectives in order to capture the richness of the information available.

Conclusion

The more sophisticated methods of evaluation require the expenditure of a good deal of energy and time. The costs can be heavy and, if this is to be justified as an investment, some selection of programmes is indicated. Some training events are essentially social (for example, the one-day get-together where people from different functions meet and hear a series of briefings on the work of other parts of the organization). Evaluation of such events would hardly be worth the cost involved.

The importance of the programme is a further criterion for consideration. Usually, evaluation of one-off programmes would not be considered worth while. However, if the programme is intended to help with the solution of some important problem, evaluation is indicated. Similarly, if the consequences of not ensuring that the training has been effective (for instance, with safety training) are important, evaluation should be considered.

It is my view that evaluation *should* be required of *any* organizational activity which represents a significant investment of funds. The costs of *not* evaluating, and thus continuing to run programmes which have no benefit, can be severe. Traditionally, evaluation has not been required of the training department, but it is becoming increasingly common for senior managers to discuss the need for training and development to contribute to business performance.

It is also necessary to recognize the political nature of evaluations. Organizations are usually comprised of groups of people with rather different interests whose views on the importance of training and development will vary. Their opinions are often based upon information which is passing informally around the organizational networks. Formal evaluative data can challenge their opinions if this is thought necessary.

Just how difficult it will be to set up a comprehensive evaluation policy will depend upon where you are starting from, what you already have in place. Below is a list of questions for you to consider. Having read this book, you probably know what the answers should be, but I suggest that you stand back and look at your existing practice.

Q1   How are the trainees selected for programmes?

a   I am not sure
b   They, or their managers, feel that the programme would be good for them
c   The training will be of direct benefit in increasing their ability either to do a particular job or to meet objectives.

Q2   What briefing do the trainees receive before the programmes?

a   Information on timing, location and general aims is sent to them
b   They receive a detailed programme of topics and the objectives for them
c   They have the opportunity to discuss with their line manager and a trainer exactly what learning will be available on the programme and how it is to be applied in the job.

Q3   Most of our programmes are aimed at:

a   A group of people (like all junior managers doing a set topic like 'Principles of Management')
b   Individuals to increase personal knowledge or change attitudes
c   Improving effectiveness in the organization.

Q4   Pre-programme evaluation or cost benefit comparisons of various methods of achieving changes are:

a   Virtually never done
b   Occasionally done
c   Frequently done, almost as a matter of course.

Q5   How do your trainers get feedback on their performance?

a   They feel good when they have performed well
b   There are reactions sheets and end-of-course discussions
c   They actually see that people are using in their jobs what they learned on the course.

Q6   When a trainee returns to the workplace, his or her manager:

a   Probably doesn't ask about the programme at all
b   Asks if he or she had a good time and whether the course was well run
c   Requires a debrief on what has been learned and becomes actively involved in making opportunities to use the learning.

Q7   Benefits from training programmes are communicated:

a   Only if requested
b   To the head of personnel and sometimes to heads of other departments
c   On a routine basis to selected audiences.

Q8   Training expenditure has to be justified by:

a   The training department
b   Heads of the various other departments
c   Line managers.

Q9   Line management involvement in the delivery of training is:

a   Nil
b   A few heads of department introduce courses and a few specialists have some input
c   Common, more than half of the programmes have some input from line managers.

Q10 At present, the training department's impact on organizational effectiveness:

a   Is not assessed because of the expense/difficulty
b   Is only assessed for one or two programmes
c   Is estimated on a regular basis.

Q11 Where does training take place?

a   Training takes place in the training department
b   Training is carried out by trainers but often in departments and sections
c   Development is a continuous activity with self-development plans and individual learning contracts. Thus training is integrated with on-the-job learning.

Q12 How is the training linked to the business?

a   Training is not linked to organizational goals
b   Training is linked to goals through an HR strategy
c   Learning is linked to organizational strategy and what individuals need in order to achieve business plans.

Scoring: 1 for an A, 2 for a B and 3 for a C.

Low scores are symptomatic of a training process in which efficiency of delivery is the main focus. It is quite likely that the trainers are good at running the activities which they have developed and will get good trainee reactions to their work. They are, however, somewhat isolated from the rest of the organization. Such a function could be at risk as it may well be seen primarily as a cost to the organization. When money is tight, the organization can, and will, cut the budget for a training department which demonstrates its value by contributing 'n' person/days training per year.

Higher scores on the questions above could indicate a training function which is more closely integrated into the day-to-day running of the organization. The organization cannot so easily cut a function which is manifestly contributing to organizational well-being and to increased effectiveness.

One way of increasing the score, and becoming more integrated with the business, is to introduce evaluation of training activities at effectiveness level. The evaluation will give a legitimate reason for trainers to be talking to line managers about the effectiveness of training and how it might contribute to improved performance. If there is some resistance from line managers who are 'too busy', it might be worth while trying to get them involved in the design and delivery of programmes which interest them. The quality of the events will usually be improved because of greater commitment to post-course activity and evaluation of benefits.

Responsive evaluation is a very powerful way of involving line managers in assessing the contribution made by training. My experience is that stakeholders are usually pleased to be asked to give an opinion and to take part in the debate as many have felt excluded from the decisions about what training should be providing. Building up a supportive network of line managers is well worth the effort involved.

Impact analysis is a way of involving senior managers in the debate about training priorities and can establish organizational criteria for the evaluation. The process is also likely to increase their support for training. Targeting senior managers and influencing their view of training is a sound political activity.

If you need yet another lever to break into the central, business part of the organization, you might draw attention to the 'Investors in People' material. For instance, try quoting:

'An Investor in People makes a public commitment from the top to develop all employees to achieve its business objectives.'
'The resources for training and developing employees should be clearly identified in the business plan.'
'The organization evaluates how its development of people is contributing to business goals and targets.'
'Top management understand the broad costs and benefits of developing people.'

There is also a series of questions to a would-be investor which include the following:

- Have you established procedures for evaluating the effectiveness of training in relation to business needs   yes/no
- Do these procedures link back to your training objectives and to your business plan?   yes/no
- Are the results of the evaluation made known to your line managers?   yes/no
- Are both your line managers and your trainees involved in evaluations?   yes/no
- Your evaluations assess levels of increased skills and

knowledge. Do they also note whether each trainee's
performance on-the-job has improved?   yes/no
- Are there data quantifying the business benefits of training
  and development?   yes/no

If the organization is to obtain maximum benefit from the training
function, trainers may have to become more political in their approach.
For instance, Garavan, Barnicle and Heraty (1993) suggest the
following strategies for increasing influence:

- Identify the key strategic initiatives in the organization and build
  training activities around them
- Forecast skills shortages and identify sources of skills within the
  organization
- Develop unique skills which cannot be performed by other readily
  available resources
- Produce a comprehensive training and development policy, tied to
  organizational policy and approved by senior management
- Ensure credibility by competence, professionalism, business
  orientation and clarity of goals (and, I would add, by evaluating and
  publishing the reports)
- Set up networks in which you are perceived as experts.

Sloman (1994) also believes that influencing skills, alliances and
coalitions are necessary. He extracts a description of best training
practice (from a survey of successful companies) which includes the
following:

- Written explicit training plans, often linked to a broader programme
  of change within the organization
- Regular written reports to the board and feedback from line
  managers on the impact and relevance of training
- A clear link between performance management and the identification
  of training needs
- Widespread evaluation of the impact of training events
- Tighter management of the training function, leading to a much
  sharper focus.

Having reached the end of the book and, I hope, identified a
number of useful ideas, you might try to draw up an action plan.
Why not select some developmental activity, on- or off-job, to
evaluate?

Aspects which need to be considered will include:

1 The cost of evaluating versus the likely benefits to:
   (a) the development of trainers
   (b) the improvement of the programme
   (c) future trainees
   (d) the relationship with line managers.

2 The potential value of the evaluation data.
3 The likely impact of the programme on organizational goals and targets.
4 The resources available to conduct evaluation.

Data will need to be collected on most of the following:

1   What is the rationale for selecting training as (part of) the solution?
2   How are the participants being selected? How close is this to a 'just-in-time' process?
3   How are the training needs linked to improvements in performance at individual, team and department level?
4   How are the expected improvements related to the business plans?
5   How are the developmental objectives agreed between the participants and their manager (and trainers?) before the activity?
6   How is the level of pre-training knowledge and skills measured?
7   How is the activity structured to build on learning from experience by reflection and then trying new ideas and skills in realistic settings?
8   How are the organizational values embedded in the activity?
9   How is the activity structured to increase self-efficacy, encourage goal-setting and increase the likelihood of transfer?
10 What evidence is there that learning of new knowledge and skills has occurred?
11 What happens after the activity to encourage the transfer of learning into new behaviours?
12 What evidence is there of changed behaviours in the workplace? How do these relate to the agreed objectives?
13 What evidence is there of increased effectiveness in the part of the organization where the participants work? How much of this is quantifiable? How does it relate to business plans? How does it relate to continuous development within the organization?
14 Do the benefits, both quantifiable and non-quantifiable, justify the cost of the activity?

A further consideration is, who is to receive the report and what process will be used?

For each stage of the proposed evaluation set a time for completion and try to analyse what (or who) is likely to hinder the achievement of that stage. It is also worth considering what you can do to mobilize support to overcome these possible hurdles.

I hope that by ending with a plan of action I have achieved what I set out to do—to write a book which not only looks at the theoretical aspects of evaluating training effectiveness, but which offers a framework for practitioners to translate theory into practice.

Appendix 1
Analysing test scores

Item analysis

Testing is always time-consuming. It is important to be sure that the time spent is effectively used. One method of avoiding time-wasting is to eliminate ineffective test items.

- Each item in the test should be directly related to a training objective.
- Each item should be of proven worth, i.e. tested and found acceptable before it is used.
- Each item found effective should be 'banked' for later use.

Facility

The *facility value (FV)* is calculated in order to answer the question, 'How easy/difficult is the item?' *FV* is the proportion of candidates who answered the item correctly.

Example: A question with four alternative responses is set to 36 trainees. The following results are obtained:

Response	A	B	C	D	Total
Totals	17	10	5	4	36

(a) The correct response is B

(b) $FV = \dfrac{10}{36} = 0.28$

(Note: Facility values should be calculated correct to two decimal places.)

(c) The facility value is very low; most have the wrong answer. Consider picking out the answer with a pin. One would expect 1 in 4 to be correct, i.e. $FV = 0.25$. The item is thus too difficult for the trainees and three questions should be asked (see Figure A1.1).

There is no clear answer to the question, 'What range of facility values is acceptable?'

(a) If we are expecting trainers to achieve objectives we need facility values of 0.70 or higher. If more than 30 per cent are answering the item incorrectly, something is wrong.

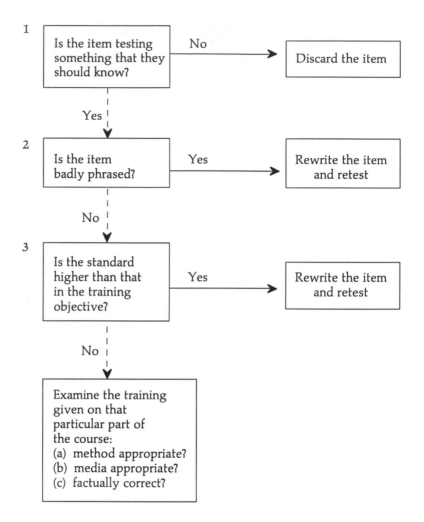

A1.1 *Item analysis*

(b) If we want to discriminate between candidates, the best range is from 0.30 to 0.70.

Discrimination   If a test item is playing its part, the good student will tend to get it correct and the poor student will tend to get it wrong. This tendency can be given a value—*the index of discrimination*—which falls between − 1 and + 1.

The *discrimination index (ID)* is usually calculated from the proportion of the top 27 per cent who answered correctly minus the proportion correct in the bottom 27 per cent. To take the example above of 36 answers to an item:

(a) 27% of 36 is approximately 10
$$\frac{36 \times 27}{100} = 9.72$$

(b) The group is then split into top 10 on the test as a whole, the bottom 10 and a middle group (see Table A1.1).

(c) The proportions correct are now calculated:
    (i)   top 27%   4 correct out of 10
$$\frac{4}{10} = 0.40$$
    (ii) bottom 27%   2 correct out of 10
$$\frac{2}{10} = 0.20$$

(d) The *ID* is then given by:
$$ID = 0.40 - 0.20$$
$$= 0.20$$

Table A1.1   *Calculating the index of discrimination*

Response	A	B*	C	D	Total
Top 10 on whole test	3	4	2	1	10
Middle 16	9	4	2	1	16
Bottom 10 on whole test	5	2	1	2	10
Totals	17	10	5	4	36

(B* is the correct response)

(e) This is a low *ID*. The top group show little more understanding than the bottom group and this is clearly unsatisfactory.

The figure of 27 per cent has been chosen as it gives the optimal size groups for discriminating, allowing for (1) maximizing the index and (2) using as much information as is possible given the constraint of (1). A reference for this is Kelley (1939).

The *ID* should never be negative—this would mean that the poorer trainees were more likely to get it correct. It cannot, however, be high with items which have high facility values—almost all the group will have answered the item correctly and there will be very little difference between the proportions.

Table A1.2   *Minimum values for ID*

FV	ID (min)
0.9	0.1
0.8	0.2
0.7	0.3
0.6	0.4
0.5	0.5
0.4	0.4
0.3	0.3

The minimum values for the *ID* recommended for differing facility bands are given in Table A1.2. If the *ID* falls below these values the item is faulty and needs rewriting.

Distractors   When using multichoice questions it is useful to examine the incorrect responses also. To take the 36 trainees tested on the four-response choice item in Table A1.1:

(a) The distractor A has attracted almost half of the group. This is probably the key to the low facility value for the item. Either the instruction has misled them or the item is badly constructed, i.e. the phraseology of A is such that it seems correct to many students.

(b) The distractors C and D are both useful, attracting a few of the group. C has a positive index of discrimination, but with such small numbers this is probably meaningless. With larger numbers this would be a cause for worry as it means that good students are more likely to pick this distractor.

Item banking   It is wasteful not to keep for later use items which have acceptable *FV*s and *ID*s. They can be kept in an item bank on a card with a format like that in Figure A1.2. The question is written on the front and the rest of the information, in pencil, on the back.

Training objective

No ....   Item No ....

	A	B*	C	D	Total
Top 27%					
Middle					
Bottom 27%					
Totals					

FV = ...   *ID* = ...

Given to Course no   ...   .

Note: B is given a * to show that that is the correct answer.

Figure A1.2   *Item banking card*

Comparing groups

Sometimes we wish to compare two sets of scores to discover whether two courses produce the same results or if one course is superior.

Suppose Course A is trained on a CBL package while Course B follows the traditional course. The courses were matched for age, sex and pre-test knowledge. Their results on the post-test are:

Students

Course A	A_1	A_2	A_3	A_4	A_5	A_6	A_7	Mean
	82	78	79	92	77	72	87	81
Course B	B_1	B_2	B_3	B_4	B_5	B_6	B_7	Mean
	80	86	65	73	64	80	63	73

The simplest method of finding out is by visual inspection. Plot the scores on a base-line.

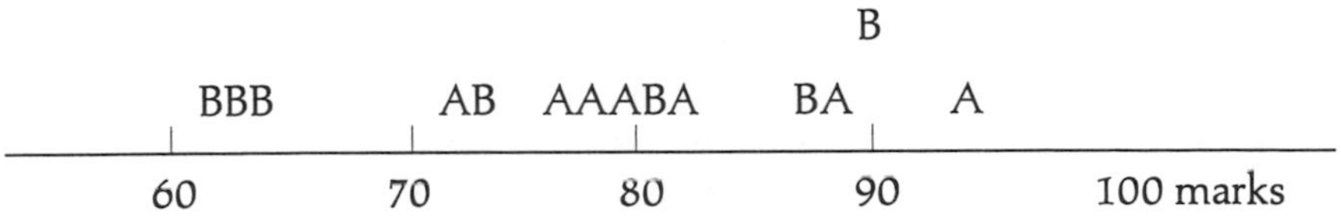

```
                                    B
      BBB          AB   AAABA     BA      A
   |_____|_____|_____|_____
   60         70         80         90         100 marks
```

There is some overlap between the two groups. If there was no overlap group A would obviously be superior, e.g.:

	BBBB	BB	B AAA A AAA

| 60 | 70 | 80 | 90 | 100 marks |

If the score were completely mixed there would be no difference between groups, e.g.:

	BAB	ABAB	A	BABABA

| 60 | 70 | 80 | 90 | 100 marks |

What we need as the basis for our decision is some measure of the amount of overlap—a large overlap means no difference, a small overlap means some difference. The method used was devised by Wilcoxon and developed by Mann-Whitney.

Table A1.3   *Critical values of U (p $\leqslant 0.05$)*

n_1 is the smaller of the two groups

n_1 / n_2	2	3	4	5	6	7	8	9	10	11	12	13	14	15	16	17	18	19	20
3																			
4				0															
5		0	1	2															
6		1	2	4	5														
7		1	3	5	7	9													
8	0	2	4	6	8	10	13												
9	0	2	4	7	10	12	15	17											
10	0	3	5	8	11	14	17	20	23										
11	0	3	6	9	13	16	19	23	26	30									
12	1	4	7	11	14	18	22	26	29	33	37								
13	1	4	8	12	16	20	24	28	33	37	41	45							
14	1	5	9	13	17	22	26	31	36	40	45	50	55						
15	1	5	10	14	19	24	29	34	39	44	49	54	59	64					
16	1	6	11	15	21	26	31	37	42	47	53	59	64	70	75				
17	2	6	11	17	22	28	34	39	45	51	57	63	67	75	81	87			
18	2	7	12	18	24	30	36	42	48	55	61	67	74	80	86	93	99		
19	2	7	13	19	25	32	38	45	52	58	65	72	78	85	92	99	106	113	
20	2	8	13	20	27	34	41	48	55	62	69	76	83	90	98	105	112	119	127

If the figure calculated for *U* is *equal* to or *less* than that given in the body of the table, the groups are different. If the figure calculated for *U* is greater than that given in the table, the groups are not (statistically) different.

(a) Look at the plots in the first example on page 147 and calculate the number of times an A comes before a B. Start from the left.
   (i)   There are no A plots before (i.e. lower than) the first 3 Bs
      $U = 0 + 0 + 0$

(ii) There is one A plot before the fourth B
$$U = 0 + 0 + 0 + 1$$
(iii) There are 4 A plots before the fifth and sixth Bs
$$U = 0 + 0 + 0 + 1 + 4 + 4$$
(iv) There are 5 A plots before the seventh B
$$U = 0 + 0 + 0 + 1 + 4 + 4 + 5$$

(b) The amount of overlap (U) is thus:
$$U = 14$$

(c) The size of the overlap depends upon the number of people involved. Here $n_1 = n_2 = 7$

(d) The critical value for U given in Table A1.3 for $n_1 = n_2 = 7$ is 9

(e) The value which we have calculated (14) is greater than 9. Therefore, the groups are not statistically different.

The decision criterion used in constructing Table A1.3 is the probability value 20 to 1 (0.05).

Reliability

People responsible for assessing trainees should keep it in mind that tests are at best imperfect measuring instruments of trainees' abilities or performance. Throughout all phases of the setting, administering and marking of tests the emphasis should be on ways and means of increasing the reliability of test scores.

An essential quality of any measuring instrument is that of reliability. In other words, reliable or consistent results ought to emerge from its use. In the assessment situation, there is little point in using a device which may fluctuate or vary with time. Ideally, one would hope that a test, for instance, when administered to two groups of very similar standards, would yield very similar results or, when administered to the same group subsequently, would produce very similar results.

Causes of low reliability

If an examiner sets and scores two different tests in the same subject, the trainees being tested are likely to obtain different scores on the two occasions.

Also, scores obtained by individual trainees in the same test are likely to show discrepancies when it is assessed by two examiners.

The main causes of poor reliability are:

(a) Changes in mental and physical states of the trainees which affect performance.
(b) Inconsistencies in the standards of scoring adopted by different examiners or by the same examiner on different occasions.
(c) Errors in scoring.
(d) Errors due to guessing.
(e) Incomplete sampling of the trainees' knowledge.

Absolute reliability will not be achieved. What is sought, therefore, is a reasonable level of reliability.

Reliability will be improved by:

(a) Increasing the length of the test—taking a larger, more adequate sample of training objectives.
(b) Maintaining standardized physical conditions, instructions and so forth.
(c) Ensuring that instructions are clear and unambiguous.
(d) Ensuring objective scoring by 'trained observers' or specialists or the use of marking guides.

Estimating the reliability of the scores

Test reliability can be assessed in two ways:

(a) Test a group of trainees twice and compare the results—test/retest.
(b) Compare the results on one half of the test with those on the other half—split half.

Test/retest reliability

If a test is reliable one would expect a trainee who scored a high mark on it today to score a high mark on it again. Similarly, people who score poor marks on the test could be expected to score poor marks on a second attempt. In other words, the test score on the 'test' should predict the score on the 'retest'.

Example: 10 trainees were tested and later retested on the same test. Their scores were:

Trainee	A	B	C	D	E	F	G	H	J	K
Test	11	8	4	4	7	2	10	7	4	3
Retest	10	7	5	2	6	2	9	5	3	3

These scores can be plotted on a scattergram (see Figure A1.3).

Between the extremes of perfect reliability and no reliability is a grey area and, in order to make decisions about whether the test is reliable enough, we need to calculate a correlation coefficient between the two sets of scores.

Test

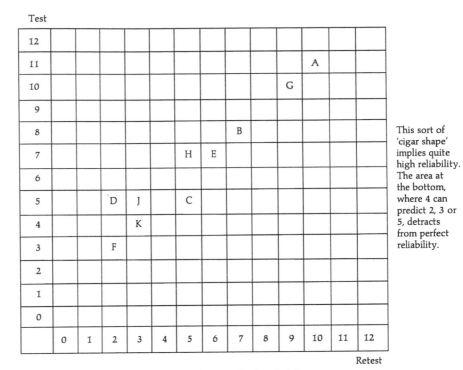

This sort of 'cigar shape' implies quite high reliability. The area at the bottom, where 4 can predict 2, 3 or 5, detracts from perfect reliability.

Retest

Figure A1.3(a)   *Scattergram showing high reliability*

Test

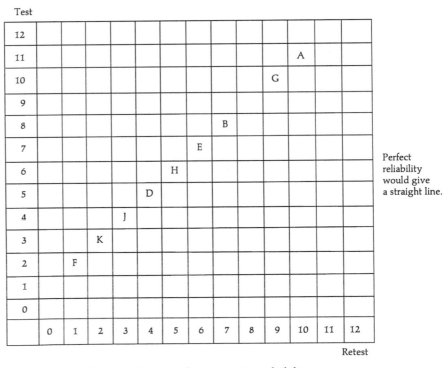

Perfect reliability would give a straight line.

Retest

Figure A1.3(b)   *Scattergram showing perfect reliability*

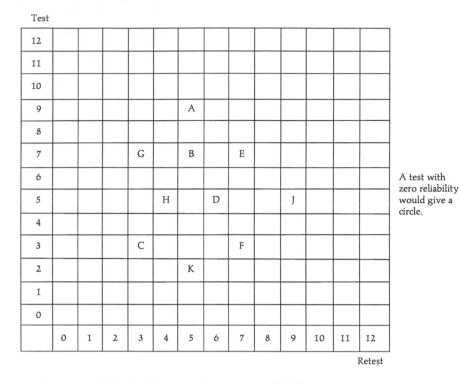

A test with zero reliability would give a circle.

Figure A1.3(c)   *Scattergram showing zero reliability*

Calculating a correlation coefficient

First plot the scattergram of the two sets of scores in Table A1.4 (see Figure A1.4).

Table A1.4   *Calculating the correlation coefficient*

Candidate	Test score	
	Test X	**Test Y**
A	92	88
B	81	79
C	57	55
D	80	78
E	73	76
F	68	76
G	80	79
H	69	65
J	61	67
K	60	53

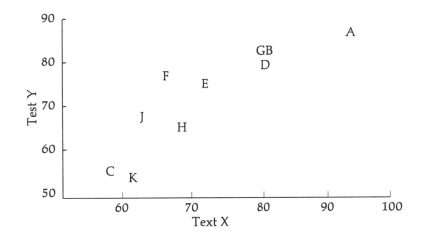

Figure A1.4 *Scattergram showing scores from tests X and Y*

Now calculate the means and draw these as a cross on the scattergram (see Figure A1.5).

$$\Sigma x = 721 \ \Sigma y = 716$$

$$x = 72.1 \ y = 71.6$$

Count the number of people in each of the four quadrants of Figure A1.6.

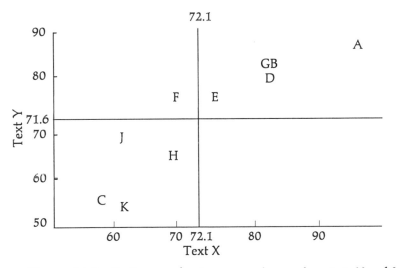

Figure A1.5 *Scattergram showing means of scores from tests X and Y*

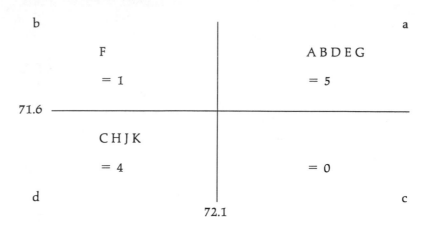

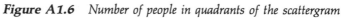

Figure A1.6 *Number of people in quadrants of the scattergram*

Cross-multiply the number of scores in opposite quadrants:

$$ad = 5 \times 4 = 20$$
$$bc = 1 \times 1^* = 1$$
$$Q = \frac{ad}{bc} = 20$$

$$r = 0.84$$

* Note: a single empty quadrant is given the value 1.

Consult Table A1.5 for various values for ad/bc.

Table A1.5   *Pearson's Qs estimates of r_{tet} for various values of ad/bc*

ad/bc	r_{tet}	ad/bc	r_{tet}	ad/bc	r_{tet}
0–1.00	0.00	2.49–2.55	0.35	8.50–8.90	0.70
1.01–1.03	0.01	2.56–2.63	0.36	8.91–9.35	0.71
1.04–1.06	0.02	2.64–2.71	0.37	9.36–9.82	0.72
1.07–1.08	0.03	2.72–2.79	0.38	9.83–10.33	0.73
1.09–1.11	0.04	2.80–2.87	0.39	10.34–10.90	0.74
1.12–1.14	0.05	2.88–2.96	0.40	10.91–11.51	0.75
1.15–1.17	0.06	2.97–3.05	0.41	11.52–12.16	0.76
1.18–1.20	0.07	3.06–3.14	0.42	12.17–12.89	0.77
1.21–1.23	0.08	3.15–3.24	0.43	12.90–13.70	0.78
1.24–1.27	0.09	3.25–3.34	0.44	13.71–14.58	0.79
1.28–1.30	0.10	3.35–3.45	0.45	14.59–15.57	0.80
1.31–1.33	0.11	3.46–3.56	0.46	15.58–16.65	0.81
1.34–1.37	0.12	3.57–3.68	0.47	16.66–17.88	0.82
1.38–1.40	0.13	3.69–3.80	0.48	17.89–19.28	0.83
1.41–1.44	0.14	3.81–3.92	0.49	19.29–20.85	0.84
1.45–1.48	0.15	3.93–4.06	0.50	20.86–22.68	0.85
1.49–1.52	0.16	4.07–4.20	0.51	22.69–24.76	0.86
1.53–1.56	0.17	4.21–4.34	0.52	24.77–27.22	0.87
1.57–1.60	0.18	4.35–4.49	0.53	27.23–30.09	0.88
1.61–1.64	0.19	4.50–4.66	0.54	30.10–33.60	0.89
1.65–1.69	0.20	4.67–4.82	0.55	33.61–37.79	0.90
1.70–1.73	0.21	4.83–4.99	0.56	37.80–43.06	0.91
1.74–1.78	0.22	5.00–5.18	0.57	43.07–49.83	0.92
1.79–1.83	0.23	5.19–5.38	0.58	49.84–58.79	0.93
1.84–1.88	0.24	5.39–5.59	0.59	58.80–70.95	0.94
1.89–1.93	0.25	5.60–5.80	0.60	70.96–89.01	0.95
1.94–1.98	0.26	5.81–6.03	0.61	89.02–117.54	0.96
1.99–2.04	0.27	6.04–6.28	0.62	117.55–169.67	0.97
2.05–2.10	0.28	6.29–6.54	0.63	169.68–293.12	0.98
2.11–2.15	0.29	6.55–6.81	0.64	293.13–923.97	0.99
2.16–2.22	0.30	6.82–7.10	0.65	923.98–	1.00
2.23–2.28	0.31	7.11–7.42	0.66		
2.29–2.34	0.32	7.43–7.75	0.67		
2.35–2.41	0.33	7.76–8.11	0.68		
2.42–2.48	0.34	8.12–8.49	0.69		

Compute $\dfrac{bc}{ad}$ if it is larger than $\dfrac{ad}{bc}$

b	a
d	c

r will then be negative

The *reliability coefficient* is an important piece of information. Tests with low coefficients do not accurately grade students. In the table below students have been graded A – E on their test results. As the reliability coefficient decreases so the proportion awarded an incorrect grade increases.

$r =$	1.00	Incorrectly graded =	0%
	0.9		23%
	0.8		33%
	0.7		40%
	0.5		50%

Decisions based upon a trainee's grades where the reliability of the test is less than 0.8 are suspect.

Split-half reliability

It is rarely possible to test and retest trainees. An alternative is to split the test into two halves—usually odd items and even items—then correlate the two halves as if they were two tests, as above.

Example: 10 trainees take a test with 40 items in it. The test is marked and the results split as below:

Candidate	Number of odd items correct (X)	Number of even items correct (Y)
A	15	12
B	19	16
C	16	17
D	18	18
E	17	20
F	16	15
G	15	10
H	14	13
J	16	14
K	19	19

Plot the candidates on a scattergram and work out the means (see Figure A1.7)

b   C   B D E K   a
        = 1   = 4

                                      $Q = \dfrac{ad}{bc}$

15.4 ───────────────┼─────────────── $= \dfrac{20}{1}$

        A F G H J $r = \underline{0.84}$
        = 5   = 0 *
d   c

* Note: A single empty quadrant is given the value 1.

Figure A1.7   *Scattergram of scores showing split-half reliability*

Appendix 2
Designing questionnaires and analysing the data

Most of the information used by evaluators is gathered by the use of structured interviews and questionnaires. There is a good deal of similarity between the two methods and the two techniques can often be combined with the evaluator administering a questionnaire on the more quantitative aspects, then following this up with an interview.

Questionnaires are used more frequently than interviews; this is due to a combination of some of the following advantages:

- Questionnaires are much cheaper; it is expensive to have interviewers travelling long distances and interviewing large numbers of people.
- Much larger samples can be taken using questionnaires and the questions can be administered to a large sample simultaneously.
- By careful design, the processing of questionnaire answers can be made very simple and efficient.
- It is often easier to convince respondents of the anonymity of their answers if they are filling in a questionnaire as opposed to undergoing a face-to-face interview.

On the other hand, questionnaires have a number of disadvantages when compared with interviews. These stem primarily from the greater flexibility within the interview situation, where the evaluator can follow leads as necessary and is not confined to the printed questions. Questionnaires are also likely to elicit response biases as respondents have a tendency to answer the questions in what they perceive to be a socially acceptable manner.

Planning the questionnaire

The most important stage in the use of a questionnaire is the planning before it is drafted. The following questions need to be answered:

- Is a questionnaire the best method of collecting the data?
- What information is required?

- Who is to provide this information?
- What type of analysis will be carried out on the information collected?

All of these questions are, of course, interlinked and decisions taken on one question may well determine the answer to other questions.

The type of information required will often determine the format of the questionnaire and this will control the analysis of the data collected. It is therefore necessary to think about this before the design stage.

The ideal sample consists of everyone who has relevant information and one of the advantages of a questionnaire approach is that this is sometimes possible. If the numbers involved are less than 200, this is probably the best strategy. If very large numbers are involved or the resources available to collect and analyse the data are limited, it may be necessary to select a sample from the total population (i.e. everyone who is of interest). If the sample is carefully drawn, it should be possible to use the data as representative of that which would have been collected had the whole population responded.

A simple random sample of respondents can be selected by procedures such as drawing numbers from a hat, taking names at regular intervals from an alphabetical list, or using tables of random numbers. If the variation of opinions within the total population is not thought to be great, a simple random sample of 20 to 30 per cent should give representative information.

If it is thought likely that there will be a wide variation in the opinion held by people in different parts of the organization or in different organizations, then a stratified sample may give a better estimate. In this, the total population is broken down into major divisions or strata, and a random sample is taken from each stratum. For instance, in following up a junior management programme, the strata could be the functions in which the people now work. Some strata will have more people in them and need a bigger sample; some will have more variation in them and again need a bigger sample.

A questionnaire can be completed either with or without supervision. The method of administration will affect the design and must be taken into account during the planning stage. Unsupervised questionnaires need very careful design and pilot runs will be necessary to eliminate ambiguities. They must also be simple. Supervised questionnaires can be more complex.

Closed questions, where the respondent is asked to select one answer from a number of alternatives, are easy to analyse and the questionnaire can be designed so that the analysis may be carried out mechanically. If the sample is large and a number of issues are to be investigated, then most of the questions should be of this type. Open-ended questions, where respondents are allowed to write in whatever they please, are very difficult to analyse. It will be necessary to establish categories so that the information can be summarized in a usable form, and this will involve a good deal of time. This must be clearly understood and anticipated at the planning stage. Open questions allow people the opportunity to express their particular point of view rather than being confined to predetermined answers. This makes some people feel more at ease. The choice of format for the questions should be governed by the sort of information required, the ease with which useful information can be extracted from the responses, and *convenience for the respondents*. The cooperation of the respondents is essential; long and complicated questionnaires will only antagonize them. It is important to try to make them 'user-friendly'.

Questionnaire construction

To ensure willing cooperation, the purpose of the questionnaire must be explained either in a written introduction or by the person administering it. Instructions on how to complete it should be simple and clear. Above all, the document should give the impression that it has been carefully prepared and produced.

Answers to early questions tend to be unreliable, so it is best to start with something factual like personal details. If response becomes mechanical, the answers again become inaccurate. It is therefore worth thinking about different sections to the document, each with a different layout.

All questions should be written in a way which helps those who are answering them to do so accurately. The questions should therefore be as short as possible and be phrased in language which the respondents will understand. The intention is not to confuse them with complicated constructions; even the use of negatives, as in the first part of this sentence, will confuse some.

Closed questions will often take up a large part of the questionnaire as they are easier for the respondent to answer and for the evaluator to analyse. The simplest form is a binary question like:

In your present job it is necessary for you to:

Diagnose mechanical faults in	Yes/No
Repair...	Yes/No
Supervise someone using	Yes/No

Where there are a number of possible answers, a polylog question can be used:

To what extent are you involved in writing proposals for ....?

☐ I write them

☐ I advise on them

☐ I make some recommendations

☐ I am not involved

Sometimes preference scales are used to assess the strength of attitudes. There are several formats for this. The best offer two opposite statements and a space for responses.

I find my work
very interesting   1   2   3   4   5   6   7   I find my work
deadly dull

The response space can be labelled rather than numbered.

Statement X	Strongly agree X	Agree X	Neutral	Agree Y	Strongly agree Y	Statement Y
The interviewer seemed very interested in me as a person						The interviewer didn't seem to be at all interested in me as a person

When it is difficult to produce opposites an agree/disagree format can be used:

Statement	Strongly agree	Agree	Undecided	Disagree	Strongly disagree
I feel that ...					
... is an important objective of my job					

Open-ended questions can often be included at the pilot stage and later converted into questions which are easier to analyse. The range of responses which are offered can be content analysed and the themes then used as categories for closed questions. For example, in the pilot we might ask, 'What topics which would be useful to you in your job were not covered on the course?' The question which would then be included in the questionnaire proper might be:

The following have been recommended as areas where extensions to the basic course would be helpful:

Technique	Do you agree?		If yes, what particularly?
	yes	no	
Network analysis			
Costing			
etc.			

The question would usually be followed by an open-ended one:

Are there other topics which you think should be included?

    Topic ...   What would you have found particularly useful?

The value in this sort of approach is that it increases the response rate. Most people will answer 'yes' or 'no' if asked, 'Do you think that X would have been useful to you?' Not many people answer questions of the type, 'What do you think ought to be done?'

The construction of the questionnaire is not complete until it has been tried on a sample of the target population and shown to give the sorts of answers which were expected. Respondents often do not interpret questions in the same way as the writer and the only way to sort out ambiguities is to ask the questions and discuss the answers. The best way to carry out the pilot is to sit with a few of the respondents and encourage them to discuss questions which are difficult to understand or to answer.

Distribution of questionnaires

Postal distribution is the most popular method, but contacting the respondents personally or through an agent is likely to produce a better response rate. As well as the questionnaire itself, there will usually be a covering letter. This should explain the purpose of the investigation and thank the respondent for the time spent in answering the questions. If there is an official sponsor of the project this should also be stated. The date by which the questionnaire is to be returned should be stated. Don't give respondents more than three weeks or they will put it to one side and forget it. If the form is to be returned by post, a stamped addressed envelope should be provided.

The intention is to get as high a response rate as possible. When less than 70 per cent of the questionnaires are returned, there must be grave doubts about whether the responses are representative. Random sampling is not achieved by low response rates.

Analysis of data

The simplest method of summarizing questionnaire data is some form of frequency statement. For example:

	Strongly agree X	Agree X	Undecided	Agree Y	Strongly agree Y	
Statement X	3	25	10	10	2	Statement Y

This represents the distribution of the opinions of 50 people on the statements X and Y.

A refinement would be to express the numbers in the boxes as percentages of the total number surveyed. In our example this would become:

	SA X	A X	Un	A Y	SA Y	
X	6%	50%	20%	20%	4%	Y

This is easier to understand when the number of people surveyed is not a round number. Percentages can be misleading if small numbers are involved. The total number surveyed should appear somewhere in the summary. It is, of course, easy to show frequencies or percentages as bar graphs if it is felt that this is likely to increase understanding.

Sometimes the opinions are reduced to a mean response for the purpose of comparisons. The boxes are given numbers and the frequencies multiplied by these. For instance, in the example above:

$$
\begin{array}{ccccc}
1 & 2 & 3 & 4 & 5 \\
\end{array}
$$

X
$$
\begin{array}{ccccc}
3 & 25 & 10 & 10 & 2
\end{array}
$$
Y

Weight $= 3 + 50 + 30 + 40 + 10$

$= 133$

Average $= 2.7$

This is a very dubious exercise. There is no reason to believe that the intervals between the boxes are equal and there is therefore no justification for using processes of multiplication or division.

If it is intended to compare one set of opinions with another, the correct method is to use the Chi-squared statistic rather than the mean response. Suppose that we have two sets of opinions extracted from two courses about a particular issue.

Statement X	Agree X	Tend to agree X	Undecided	Tend to agree Y	Agree Y	Statement Y
Course A	10	20	10	5	5	
Course B	5	10	15	5	5	

If the proportions across the boxes are similar, then there is no statistical difference between the frequencies. In this case we could estimate the frequency in any one box from the frequencies in the others and produce a figure that is quite close to the one actually found.

Estimating the frequencies in the boxes and comparing these with the actual frequencies found is the basis of the Chi-squared test. Where large differences are found, the frequencies can be said to represent different opinions or pass rates or whatever.

To take the example above. First of all, find the row and column totals:

	X		N		Y	Totals
Course A	10	20	10	5	5	50
Course B	5	10	25	5	5	50
Totals	15	30	35	10	10	100

Now calculate the 'expected value' in each cell from the formula:

$$\frac{\text{Row total} \times \text{Column total}}{\text{Overall total}}$$

For the first cell this is

$$\frac{50 \times 15}{100} = 7.5$$

For the second

$$\frac{50 \times 30}{100} = 15$$

For the third

$$\frac{50 \times 35}{100} = 17.5$$

Fill in the new block by writing the expected values in brackets underneath the actual, observed values:

10	20	10	5	5	50
(7.5)	(15)	(17.5)	(5)	(5)	
5	10	25	5	5	50
(7.5)	(15)	(17.5)	(5)	(5)	
15	30	35	10	10	100

Subtract all the expected values from the observed values and calculate Chi-squared from the formula:

$$\chi^2 = \Sigma \frac{(\text{Observed–Expected})^2}{\text{Expected}}$$

i.e.
$$\chi^2 = \frac{(10 - 7.5)^2}{7.5} + \frac{(20 - 15)^2}{15} + \frac{(10 - 17.5)^2}{17.5}$$

$$+ \frac{(5 - 5)^2}{5} + \frac{(5 - 5)^2}{5} + \frac{(5 - 7.5)^2}{7.5} + \frac{(10 - 15)^2}{15}$$

$$+ \frac{(25 - 17.5)^2}{17.5} + \frac{(5 - 5)^2}{5} + \frac{5 - 5)^2}{5}$$

$$= 0.833 + 1.667 + 3.21 + 0 + 0 + 0.833 + 1.667 + 3.21 + 0 + 0$$

$$\chi^2 = 11.42$$

The figure of 11.42 is a measure of the difference in the opinions expressed by the two courses. We must now decide whether it is large enough to discount chance variation and state that the opinions are different.

The table of critical values (Table A2.1) is based on the 1 in 20 criterion. The degrees of freedom are calculated from:

$$df = (\text{Number of rows} - 1)(\text{Number of columns} - 1)$$

In this case we have:

$$df = (2 - 1)(5 - 1) = 4$$

The critical value for *df* 4 is 9.49. The figure for χ^2 that we have calculated (11.42) is larger than this; thus we can say that the expressed opinions of the two groups are different.

Table A2.1   *Critical values for χ^2 (p $\leqslant 0.05$)*

$df = (r-1)(c-1)\chi^2$	Critical values for	$df = (r-1)(c-1)\chi^2$	Critical values for
1	3.84	20	31.41
2	5.99	21	32.67
3	7.81	22	33.92
4	9.49	23	35.17
5	11.07	24	36.42
6	12.59	25	37.65
7	14.07	26	38.89
8	15.51	27	40.11
9	16.92	28	41.34
10	18.31	29	42.56
11	19.68	30	43.77
12	21.03	40	55.76
13	22.36	50	67.50
14	23.68	60	79.08
15	25.00	70	90.53
16	26.30	80	101.9
17	27.59	90	113.1
18	28.87	100	124.3
19	30.14		

The value for χ^2 is computed from:

$$\chi^2 = \sum \frac{(0 - E)^2}{E}$$

Appendix 3
Designing interviews and analysing the data

The interview is a widely used technique for gathering evaluation data. The interviewer can ask direct questions, and further probing and clarification is possible as the interview proceeds. This flexibility is very valuable for exploring issues as it can give more depth to the investigation than is possible when using questionnaires.

Interviews may be highly structured, resembling questionnaires, but usually start with general questions to allow the respondent to talk about some of the issues which he or she feels are important. Sometimes interviews will be exploratory and will have very little pre-planned structure. An example would be the rather informal discussions of 'how things are going' which take place in the bar on residential courses.

Interviewing typically involves a one-to-one interaction, but it can be carried out with a group. Group interviews save time and allow the respondents to build on each other's responses, but this influence sometimes leads the group in a direction which none of the individuals would have chosen. The situation may also inhibit the contribution of group members as some people are inclined not to express views if they feel that they are in a minority. The empathic relationship which is the hallmark of a good interview is more difficult to achieve in a group setting. There is also the problem of the situation giving undue prominence to the statements of those who are more articulate or more confident.

Planning

The first decision to be made by the evaluator is whether interviewing is the most appropriate method of data collection. It will be particularly useful when: reappraising previously identified training needs; exploring the extent of transfer of learning; examining the effectiveness of particular training methods; and when trying to relate activities to organizational goals and purposes.

A major drawback of interviews is the time taken to conduct and analyse them. As we found with questionnaires, personal bias can distort the data. With interviews this is not only self-report bias, but also the bias of the interviewer. The type of question asked and the nature of the interaction will encourage certain kinds of responses and discourage others. Interviewing takes considerable skill if valid data are to be collected. Interviewers must understand their own biases and those of the respondents. They must also be able to listen actively and to change the shape of the interview in order to probe issues which arise. If the respondents are to raise sensitive issues and offer frank statements, it will also be necessary to establish an empathic relationship with the respondents.

The next step in planning is to decide what information is sought and thus what questions must be asked. A rough interview schedule is drafted and tested on a colleague. It is then refined and piloted with a few members of the target population. The schedule will help the interviewer by providing a reminder of the points to be explored. It should not be so detailed that it dictates the whole pattern of the interview. Interviewing should be a flexible process which allows the exploration of themes which were not anticipated when the schedule was drawn up. If it has a rigid format, the data can be more economically collected by using a questionnaire.

Questions for the schedule could include some of the following:

Questions	**Probing**
What did you hope to get out of the course before you went on it?	To find out if expectations were realistic
Did it meet your expectations?	If not, why not?
What were the most useful things that you learned?	Useful for job performance? In what way useful?
What are you doing differently since the programme?	Ask for specific examples; try to connect to learning.
Anything else?	Describe a specific incident.
Did you talk to your supervisor when you returned?	What kind of debrief? What benefit from it?

Specific questions can be asked about particular aspects of the programme; ask what candidates thought were its strengths or weaknesses; ask about aspects which were new or had been tried for the first time, etc:

Is there anything else that you would like to say about the programme?

Is there anything that we
haven't talked about that you
think we should have talked
about?

Contracting Establishing a good relationship with the interviewee is the purpose of
the early part of the interview. What should happen is that a form of
contract is negotiated. The interviewee will have questions (although
these may not be asked) and the answers to them will form the basis of
the contract. Areas which should be discussed will include:

- Who am I? Why am I here? What are my goals?
- Who am I working for?
- What do I want from you and what am I going to do with the
  information?
- Who will see the data and in what format will they then be?
- How will I protect your confidentiality?

There is a further question about whether the interviewee believes that
the investigator can be trusted. A powerful aid to building a trusting
relationship is for the interviewer to provide short factual summaries
during the interview. The interviewee can then be assured that the
interviewer is at least listening to what is being said and has
understood it. It is, of course, also possible for the interviewee to
correct any misunderstanding and thus become an active participant in
the recording of the data.

Data gathering

The interview will often fall into two parts: an initial exploratory phase
of rather general discussion, and a second phase during which specific
issues are pursued. This order is recommended as it makes it more likely
that the interviewee will raise issues rather than being confined only to
the areas which he or she thinks that the interviewer is interested in.

Recording information with a highly structured interview is a simple
process of making short notes in the spaces left on the schedule. Less
structured interviews pose more difficult problems. Taking notes is the
most common method and, with practice, this will record most of the
useful information. Key words, phrases and quotes are recorded during
the interview and these are expanded before the next interview can
interfere with the memory. Taking detailed notes during the interview
will interfere with the flow and with the rapport. Few interviewees
enjoy talking to the top of someone's head.

It is possible to use a tape recorder; this has the advantage of providing
a complete record of the interview. However, this procedure will inhibit
some interviewees. Many people are wary of making statements on
sensitive issues when these can be played back verbatim somewhere
else. A further disadvantage of this method is the length of time taken

to access the information. For an interview lasting one hour, it will take about two hours to extract the main points from the recording and about four hours to make a complete transcription.

While carrying out the interview, the sensitive interviewer will realize the importance of his or her own behaviour in controlling that of the interviewee. For instance, people who avoid eye contact and regularly avert their gaze when speaking are usually suspected of being 'economical with the truth'. However, such gaze aversion can easily be induced by an interviewer who sits too close to the interviewee. Similarly, people who make false starts to sentences and then rephrase what they were going to say are often suspected of embroidering the story. Such behaviour can easily be induced by an interviewer who has too much eye contact and who is thus perceived to be an interrogator.

Talking is often seen as active and listening as being passive. However, effective listening is an active combination of hearing, checking understanding, clarifying contradictions and summarizing what has been said. It also requires some commitment to exploring the respondent's viewpoint in as unbiased a way as possible. We all have preconceived ideas based upon experience, personal values, expectations of other people and untested prejudices. All of these can filter and distort what is heard. The more aware the interviewer is of these elements, the better able he or she will be to control biases in what is recorded. Reflective summaries provide an opportunity to check and correct distortions of the messages being offered. Many programmes designed to train interviewers use video recordings for feedback. This is one area where such feedback can be particularly valuable, allowing people to see for themselves just how biased they are.

Termination

Towards the end of the interview it is good practice to briefly restate some of the main themes and give the interviewee an opportunity to add additional comments. Some open-ended questions such as, 'Is there anything that you think I should have asked about, but haven't?' will sometimes uncover topics which have been overlooked. A little caution is in order here as some interviewees will take this opportunity to open floodgates. It may be worth while prefacing the question with, 'I'd like to use the last few minutes . . .'.

The interviewee should be allowed the opportunity to ask questions. There may, for instance, still be some doubts about the purpose of the interview or the level of confidentiality. The interview should be ended properly by expressing thanks. This carries through the good atmosphere in which the interview should have taken place and a statement which shows that the interviewer values the respondent's contribution helps to create goodwill.

Data analysis

Interviews can yield large amounts of information and this will need summarizing. This can be done by extracting short quotations which are thought to be representative, or by writing a short passage which is a summary of the main themes which were discussed. More often, a number of interviews are summarized for a report which will have main themes. The summary then becomes a mixture of statistical statements and more qualitative information.

Forty-three of the 57 managers interviewed had not had a debriefing session with their supervisor on return from the programme. In the 14 cases where debriefing had occurred, the benefits were reported as being:

Creation of opportunities to use new skills (9 cases)
Negotiation of the possibilities for progressing the action plan (6 cases)
More open relationship with the supervisor (4 cases)
Opportunity to discuss further development (3 cases)

Direct quotations have great impact and sometimes will be the only part which the reader remembers. Therefore, they should be used sparingly and more often when they represent a widely held view. A well-turned phrase which represents the view of only one respondent may distort the understanding of the report.

Appendix 4
Observing as an evaluative technique

One of the most direct methods of collecting evaluative data is by observing people in their work setting. The observation may be unstructured, with the person who is observing being as open-minded as possible and using his or her judgement about which events are considered important. Alternatively, it may be highly structured by the use of coded schedules which guide attention to specific types of event. The latter is more likely in evaluations of training. The categories which are selected will be those where changes are expected as a result of training, or those which are thought to be particularly important to the success of the job. In practice, the observer will often use both of these approaches, as an open-ended method can complement the rather narrow field observed with a highly structured one. Sometimes the observer will start with a relatively unstructured approach and later focus on aspects which seem to be of importance. This is the approach which Parlett and Hamilton (1977) have called 'progressive focusing'.

The recording of the information may be done during the observation or immediately after it. The former is better for detail and the latter for overall impressions. The longer the interval between the observation and the recording, the less accurate the information will be. If it is intended to quote actual statements these must be recorded faithfully and in quotation marks. There may be a case for using a tape recorder to ensure accuracy in such cases. Tape recorders may well introduce problems into the situation because those being observed are less likely to act naturally when they know that they are being recorded. People do get used to them, and after a while forget that they are there, but this may not happen in a short session.

Observations are free from the biases of self-reports in interviews or questionnaires because the evaluator is directly connected with behaviour rather than someone's perceptions of it. However, the evaluator must be sensitive to the situation and the likelihood that his or her presence will distort the performance being observed. Also, the same hazards apply as in interviewing if the observer is biased and sees only what he or she expects or wants to see.

Observing interpersonal skills of individuals

If used correctly, observations can be particularly helpful in examining interpersonal skills and relationships with others. In observing the interactions of an individual with colleagues or customers, a set of categories like those developed by Rackham and Morgan (1977) can be used. The 13 types of behaviour are listed on a sheet of paper and the frequency with which they are used in some significant period of time is recorded. Specific instances of appropriate or inappropriate use of a particular category are also recorded to be used as feedback. The categories are shown in Figure 10.1. After familiarization with the use of these, the observer could work with a sheet like Table A4.1.

Table A4.1   *Categories for observing individual interactions*

Behaviour	Frequency	Specific incidents
Proposing		
Building		
Supporting		
Disagreeing		
Defending/attacking		
Blocking/difficulty stating		
Open behaviour		
Testing understanding		
Summarizing		
Seeking information		
Giving information		
Shutting out		
Bringing in		

(*Source: Rackham and Morgan 1977*)

It is common experience that two people observing the same event will later give different accounts of it. Putting in a lot of structure by using a checklist like the one above will control some of this, but it will still be necessary to practise in order to produce reliable observations.

Observing groups at work

Interpersonal relationships are a key component of working in groups and observing interactions within the group setting can provide useful information about the nature of those relationships.

Broad categories like the following will reveal many of the important aspects:

Interruptions
- Who interprets the most, and the least?
- Who is interrupted the most, and the least?

Air space
- Who talks most, and who least?
- Who attempts to dominate the conversation?

Disagreement
- How often do they disagree?
- How do they settle disagreements?

Support
- How often do they support each other?
- Who supports whom?

If the purpose of the group is to make decisions, a checklist like Table A4.2 might be useful.

Observing a training session

One important use of observation within an evaluative strategy is the observation of training sessions. This has three main phases: some discussion with the trainer before the session, the observation itself, and some feedback afterwards.

During the pre-observation discussion, the trainer is asked what he or she is trying to achieve, i.e. for aims and objectives. The trainer is then asked to describe the shape of the session and why the specific methods have been chosen. Some discussion should occur about how the observational record will be used, to what extent the information is confidential, and to whom. It is also good practice to ask the trainer if there are any specific aspects of the session on which he or she would like feedback.

During the session the observer should be as unobtrusive as possible. Sometimes observers become active participants in the session, but this can be difficult for the trainer and it will also make it very difficult for the observer to record information. Notes should be made during the session with some detail on specific incidents. Some framework will usually be necessary in order to classify incidents. One which we have found useful is shown in Table A4.3 (see page 174). Under 'further comments' the following questions might be addressed:

- To what extent did the methods seem suitable for *this* group?
- What form of assessment of trainee progress was being used?
- How was feedback given to the trainees?

The post-observation feedback should occur as soon as possible after the session. This should begin by asking the trainer what he or she

Table A4.2   *Decision making in groups*

Who provided the structure?	Group member					
	A	B	C	D	E	F
● Follows the structure provided by others						
● Provided a plan for meeting goals which was discussed						
● Provided a plan for reaching decisions which was implemented						
How was information given?						
● Gave incorrect information or withheld something important						
● Gave information in a disorganized fashion						
● Gave information which was relevant and concise						
Who made the decision?						
● Avoided making decisions, accepted others' decisions						
● Proposed solutions for others to approve (or disapprove)						
● Proposed the solutions which were implemented						
Investment of energy						
● Low—kept silent except when asked something						
● Moderate—active for much of the time						
● High—the most active group member						

thought of the actual session compared with that expected and planned. The observer should then discuss specific incidents and how they were seen by observer, trainees and trainer. This works best when incidents where things went well are discussed first. People are generally more inclined to accept the observer's opinion when discussion of positive events precedes that of incidents when things did not go well (Stone,

Table A4.3   *Trainer appraisal form*

Name of trainer: ....   Title of session: ....

Length: ....

Place an 'X' in the box is you feel that area needs improvement, and please elaborate with comments.

Signposting	X	Comments
Introduced subject		
Referred to objectives		
Indicated main stages		
Summarized to consolidate stages		
Explained procedures		
Use of aids		
Flipchart		
Whiteboard		
Overhead projector		
Computer demonstration		
Other		
Delivery technique		
Voice (volume, tone, pace)		
Listened		
Use of questions		
Group involvement		
Checked understanding		
Eye contact		
Mannerisms		
Control		
Allocated time well		
Maintained good pace		
Kept to subject		
Overall impression		
Knowledgeable		
Enthusiastic		
Aware of group needs		
Created interest		

Any further comments:

Observer: Date:

Guertal and McIntosh, 1984). Whatever the purpose of the observation, the feedback is intended to be a helpful reflection for the trainer and it should not be heavily judgemental.

A video camera in the background can support observations. This has the advantage of full data which can later be observed by more than one person and thus be impartially classified. This is often useful for feedback during the training of interviewers, trainers, etc. as they can afterwards see how they appear to others. It may also be suitable for research and for training in observation skills. However, it is time-consuming and may not be a cost-effective method of gathering evaluative data.

Selected bibliography

A few books and articles which I have found particularly interesting are listed below.

Goldstein, A.P. and M. Sorcher (1974) *Changing Supervisor Behaviour*, Pergamon Press, New York.

An excellent example of the old adage: 'there is nothing so practical as a good theory'. They take the findings of research in social learning theory and apply them to supervisory training. The work has had a major influence on the development of behavioural modelling as a training technique. As this is one of the few methods of changing interpersonal skills which has been shown to be successful, the basic source material is well worth studying. The book is out of print, but copies are available in some libraries. One of the better studies following the lead of Goldstein and Sorcher is:

Latham, G.P. and L.M. Saari (1979) 'The application of Social Learning Theory to training supervisors through behavioural modelling', *Journal of Applied Psychology*, 64, 239–246.

Rackham, N. and T. Morgan (1977) *Behavioural Analysis in Training*, McGraw-Hill, Maidenhead.

Another impressive text on interpersonal skills training. A useful review of why most interpersonal skills training doesn't result in changes in behaviour and many examples of the use of behaviour categories to achieve such change. Again, sadly, this book is out of print and only available in libraries.

Mathieu, J.E., J.W. Martineau and S.I. Tannenbaum (1993) 'Individual and situational influences on the development of self-efficacy: Implications for training effectiveness', *Personnel Psychology*, 46, 125–147.

A review paper which represents the most recent work on self-efficacy. This perception may be the crucial variable intervening between learning and changes in behaviour.

Guba, E.G. and Y.S. Lincoln (1989) *Fourth Generation Evaluation*, Sage, California.

This describes various approaches to evaluation and then argues that responsive evaluation is superior to previous strategies. They do tend to protest too much, but the book gives a good feel for what it is like to carry out a responsive evaluation.

Patton, M.C.E. (1978) *Utilization-focused Evaluation*, Sage, Beverly Hills.

Sound, practical advice for would-be evaluators. As the title suggests, he takes the view that evaluation is a political process.

Tannenbaum, S.I. and G. Yukl (1992) 'Training and development in work organizations', *Annual Review of Psychology*, 43, 399–441.

A very thorough review of recent research on aspects of training. It is not light reading, but *Annual Review* articles are always scholarly and good sources of articles which you might want to seek out and read for yourself.

References

Adams, J.A. (1987) 'Historical review and appraisal of research on the learning, retention and transfer of human motor skills', *Psychological Bulletin*, **101**, 1, 41–74.

Alliger, G.M. and E.A. Janak (1989) 'Kirkpatrick's levels of training criteria: Thirty years later', *Personnel Psychology* 42, 331–342.

Baldwin, T.T. and J.K. Ford (1988) 'Transfer of training: A review and directions for future research', *Personnel Psychology*, 41, 63–105.

Bandura, A. (1977) *Social Learning Theory*, Prentice-Hall, Englewood Cliffs, N.J.

Bandura, A. (1986) *Social Foundations of Thought and Action*, Prentice-Hall, Englewood Cliffs, N.J.

Belbin, R.M. (1981) *Management Teams: Why they Succeed or Fail*, Heinemann, London.

Berger, M. (1977) 'Training and the organizational context', *Journal of European Industrial Training*, 1, 2, 7–12.

Blake, R.R. and J.S. Mouton (1964) *The Managerial Grid*, Gulf, Houston.

Blake, R.R. and J.S. Mouton (1969) *Building a Dynamic Corporation through Grid Organization Development*, Addison-Wesley, Reading, Mass.

Bolt, J.F. (1987) 'Trends in management training and executive education', *Journal of Management Development*, 6, 5–15.

Boruch, R.F., A.J. McSweeney and E.J. Soderstrom (1978) 'Randomised Field Experiments, *Evaluation Quarterly*, 2, 655–695.

Bramley, P. (1994) 'Using subordinate appraisals as feedback', paper given to the 23rd International Congress of Applied Psychology, Madrid. Copies available from the Department of Organizational Psychology, Birkbeck College, University of London.

Bramley, P. and B. Kitson (1994) 'Evaluating against business criteria', *Journal of European Industrial Training*, **18**, 1, 10–14.

Byham, W.C. (1982) 'How assessment centers are used to evaluate training effectiveness', *Training*, (The Magazine of Human Resource Development), February.

Cameron, K. (1980) 'Critical questions in assessing organizational effectiveness', *Organizational Dynamics*, Autumn, 66–80.

Cascio, W.F. (1982) *Costing Human Resources: The Financial Impact of Behaviour in Organizations*, Kent, Boston.

Chapple, E.D. and L.R. Sayles (1961) *The Measurement of Managements*, Macmillan, New York.

Constable, J. and R. McCormick (1987) *The Making of British Managers*, BIM, CBI, London.

Cook, J.D., S.J. Hepworth, T.D. Wall and P.B. Warr (1981) *The Experience of Work*, Academic Press, London.

Cronbach, L.J. (1982) *Designing Evaluations of Educational and Social Programmes*, Jossey-Bass, San Francisco.

Dale, B.G. and T.S. Ball (1983) *A Study of Quality Circles in UK Manufacturing Organizations*, Department of Management Sciences, UMIST, Manchester.

Dale, B.G. and S.G. Hayward (1984) 'Some reasons for quality circle failure', *Leadership and Organizational Development Journal*, Parts I, II and III.

Davies, I.K. (1971) *The Management of Learning*, McGraw-Hill, London.

Donnison, P.A. (1993) *The Effect of Outdoor Management Development on Self-efficacy*, unpublished MSc dissertation, Birkbeck College, University of London.

Dunnette, M.D. and L.M. Hough (1992) (eds) *Handbook of Industrial and Organizational Psychology*, (2nd edition), Consulting Psychologists Press, Palo Alto.

Easterby-Smith, M. (1986) *Evaluation of Management Education, Training and Development*, Gower, Aldershot.

Easterby-Smith, M. (1994) *Evaluation of Management Education, Training and Development* (2nd edition), Gower, Aldershot.

EFQM (1993) *Total Quality Management: The European Model for Self-Appraisal*, Fellenoord 47A, Eindhoven, The Netherlands.

Faley, R.H. and E. Sandstrom (1985) 'Content representativeness: an empirical method of evaluation', *Journal of Applied Psychology*, 70, 567–571.

Ford, J.K. and S.P. Wroten (1984) 'Introducing new methods for conducting training evaluation and for linking training evaluation to program design', *Personnel Psychology* 37, 651–656.

Fournier, V. (1994) 'Cognitive maps and workrole transition', paper given to the 23rd International Congress of Applied Psychology, Madrid, July.

Gagne, R.M. (1970) *The Conditions of Learning*, Holt, Rinehart and Winston, New York.

Garavan, T.N., B. Barnicle and N. Heraty (1993) 'The training and development function: Its search for power and influence in organizations', *Journal of European Industrial Training*, **17**, 7, 22–32.

Georgeopolous, B.S. and A.S. Tannenbaum (1957) 'The study of organizational effectiveness', *American Sociological Review*, 22, 534–540.

Glossary of Training Terms (1971) Department of Employment, HMSO.

Goldsmith T.E., R.S. Johnson and W.H. Acton (1991) 'Assessing structural knowledge', *Journal of Educational Psychology*, 83, 88–96.

Goldstein, A.P. and M. Sorcher (1974) *Changing Supervisor Behaviour*, Pergamon Press, New York.

Goldstein, I.L. (1992) 'Training in work organizations', Chapter 9 in M.D. Dunnette and L.M. Hough (eds), *Handbook of Industrial and Organizationl Psychology*, (2nd edition), Consulting Psychologists Press, Palo Alto.

Goldstein, I.L. (1993) *Training in Organizations* (3rd edition), Brooks/Cole, California.

Goodman, P.S. and J.W. Dean (1982) 'Creating long-term organizational change', in P.S. Goodman and Associates, *Change in Organizations*, Jossey Bass, California.

Guba, E.G. and Y.S. Lincoln (1989) *Fourth Generation Evaluation*, Sage, California.

Hagman, J. and A. Rose (1983) 'Retention of military tasks: A review', *Human Factors*, 25, 193–213.

Hamblin, A.C. (1974) *Evaluation and Control of Training*, McGraw-Hill, London.

Havelock, R.G. (1969) *Planning for Innovation through Dissemination and Utilization of Knowledge*, Institute for Social Research, University of Michigan.

Henerson, M.E., L.L. Morris and C.T. Fitzgibbon (1978) *How to Measure Attitudes*, Sage, Beverly Hills.

Hinrichs, J.R. (1976) 'Personnel training', Chapter 19 of M.D. Dunnette (ed) *Handbook of Organizational and Industrial Psychology*, Rand McNally, Chicago.

Hussey, D.E. (1985) 'Implementing corporate strategy: using management education and training', *Long Range Plan*, **18**, 5, 28–37.

Ishikawa, K. (1968) *Quality Circles Activities*, Union of Japanese Scientists and Engineers, Tokyo, Japan.

Katz, D. and R.L. Khan (1978) *The Social Psychology of Organizations*, 2nd edition, Wiley, New York.

Kearsley, E. (1982) *Costs, Benefits and Productivity in Training Systems*, Addison-Wesley, Reading, Mass.

Kelley, P. (1939) 'The selection of upper and lower groups for the validation of test items', *Journal of Education Psychology*, **224**, 30, 17–24.

Kirkpatrick, D.L. (1959) 'Techniques for evaluating training programmes', *Journal of the American Society of Training Directors*, 13, 3–9 and 21–26; 14, 13 18 and 28–32.

Kolb, D.A. (1984) *Experiential Learning*, Prentice-Hall, Englewood Cliffs, N.Y.

Latham, G.P. (1988) 'Human resource training and development', *Annual Review of Psychology*, 39, 545–582.

Latham, G.P. and L.M. Saari (1979) 'The application of social learning theory to training supervisors through behavioural modelling', *Journal of Applied Psychology*, 64, 239–246.

Legge, K. (1984) *Evaluating Planned Organizational Change*, Academic Press, London.

Leviton, L.C. and E.F.X. Hughes (1981) 'Research on the utilization of evaluations: A review and synthesis', *Evaluation Review*, 5, 525–548.

Locke, E.A. and G.P. Latham (1990) *A Theory of Goal Setting and Task Performance*, Prentice-Hall, Englewood Cliffs, N.J.

McGarrell, E.R. (1984) 'An orientation system that builds productivity', *Personnel Administrator*, **29**, 10, 75–85.

McGehee, W. and P.W. Thayer (1961) *Training in Business and Industry*, Wiley, New York.

Mager, R.F. (1962) *Preparing Objectives for Programmed Instruction*, Fearon, San Francisco.

Mager, R.F. and P. Pipe (1970) *Analysing Performance Problems*, Fearon, California.

Marx, R.D. (1982) 'Relapse prevention for managerial training', *Academy of Management Review*, 7, 27–40.

Massey, J.C. (1957) 'Postal carrier training', *Journal of the American Society for Training and Development*, September/October.

Mathieu, J.E., J.W. Martineau and S.I. Tannenbaum (1993) 'Individual and situational influences on the development of self-efficacy: Implications for training effectiveness', *Personnel Psychology*, 46, 125–147.

Mayer, S.J. and J.S. Russell (1987) 'Behavior modeling training in organizations', *Journal of Management*, 13, 21–40.

Mintzberg, H. (1992) Alec Rodger Memorial Lecture, Birkbeck College, University of London.

Mirvis, P.H. and B.A. Macy (1982) 'Evaluating program costs and benefits', Chapter 17 in E.S. Seashore, E.E. Lawler, P.H. Mirvis and C. Camman (eds), *Assessing Organizational Change*, Wiley, New York.

Morris, M. and R. Cohn (1993) 'Programme evaluators and ethical challenges: A national survey', *Evaluation Review*, **17**, 6, 621–642.

Mullen, B. and C. Cooper (1994) 'The relation between group cohesiveness and performance: an integration', *Psychological Bulletin*, 115, 210–227.

National Training Awards 1988, 1991, 1992, 1993, Sheffield S1 4PQ, Employment Department.

Newman D. (1985) *The Pursuit of Validity in Training*, unpublished doctoral dissertation, University of Maryland (quoted in Goldstein, 1992).

Parlett, M. and D. Hamilton (1977) 'Evaluation as a new approach to the study of innovative programmes', in D. Hamilton *et al* (eds), *Beyond the Numbers Game*, Macmillan, London.

Patrick, J., I. Michael and A. Moore (1986) *Design for Learning*, Occupational Services Ltd, Aston Science Park, Birmingham.

Patton, M.C.E. (1978) *Utilization-focused Evaluation*, Sage, Beverly Hills.

Pearn, M. (1981) *CRAMP: A Guide to Training Decisions*, ITRU Research paper TRI, Industrial Training Research Unit, Cambridge.

Pedler, M. (ed) (1983) *Action Learning in Practice*. Gower, Aldershot.

Porter, L.W. and L.E. McKibbin (1988) *Management Education and*

Development: Drift or Thrust into the 21st Century? McGraw-Hill, New York.

Prophet, E. (1976) *Long-term Retention of Flying Skills: A Review of the Literature*, HUMRRO/FR-EDP-76-35 (Human Resources Research Organization) Alexandria, Virginia.

Rackham, N. and T. Morgan (1977) *Behavioural Analysis in Training*, McGraw-Hill, Maidenhead.

Ralphs, L.T. and E. Stephan (1986) 'HRD in the Fortune 500', *Training and Development Journal*, 40, 69–76.

Randall, L.K. (1960) 'Evaluation: A training dilemma', *Journal of the American Society of Training Directors*, 14, 29–35.

Rossi, P.H. and H.E. Freeman (1989) *Evaluation: A Systematic Approach* (4th edition), Sage, Beverly Hills.

Sanderson, P.M., J.M. James and N. Seidler (1989) 'SHAPA: An interactive software', *Ergonomics*, 32, 1271–1302.

Sashkin M., W.C. Morris and L. Horst (1973) 'A comparison of social and organizational change models', *Psychological Review*, 50, 6.

Seashore, S.E., E.E. Lawler, P.H. Mirvis and C. Camman (1982) *Assessing Organizational Change*, Wiley, New York.

Skinner, B.F. (1954) 'The science of learning and the art of teaching', in A.A. Lumsdaine and R. Glaser (eds), *Teaching Machines and Programmed Learning*, NEA, Washington, DC.

Sloman, M. (1994) *A Handbook for Training Strategy*, Gower, Aldershot.

Solomon, M.A. and S.M. Shortell (1981) 'Designing health policy research for utilization', *Health Policy Quarterly*, 1, 261–237.

Stake, R.E. (ed) (1975) *Evaluating the Arts in Education: A Responsive Approach*, Merrill, Columbus, Ohio.

Stammers, R. and J. Patrick (1975) *The Psychology of Training*, Methuen, London.

Stewart, A. and V. Stewart (1981) *Business Applications of Repertory Grids*, McGraw-Hill, Maidenhead.

Stone, D.L., H.G. Guertal and B. McIntosh (1984) 'The effects of feedback sequence and expertise of the rater on perceived feedback accuracy', *Personnel Psychology*, 37, 487–506.

Sykes, A.J.M. (1962) 'The effect of a supervisory training course on supervisors' perceptions and expectations of the role of management', *Human Relations*, 15, 227–244.

Tannenbaum, S.I., R.L. Beard and E. Sales (1992) 'Team building and its influence on team effectiveness: an examination of conceptual and empirical developments', in K. Kelley (ed), *Issues, Theory and Research in Industrial/Organizational Psychology*, North Holland, London.

Tannenbaum, S.I. and G. Yukl (1992) 'Training and development in work organizations', *Annual Review of Psychology*, 43, 399–441.

Training in Britain: A Study of Funding, Activity and Attitudes (1989) HMSO, London.

Tyler, R.W. (1950) *Basic Principles of Curriculum and Instruction Design*, University of Chicago Press, Chicago.

van de Vall, M. and C.A. Bolas (1981) 'External versus internal social policy researchers', *Knowledge: Creation, Diffusion, Utilization*, 2, 461–481.

van Fleet, D.D. and R.W. Griffin (1989) 'Quality circles: A review and suggested future directions', *International Review of Industrial and Organizational Psychology*, 7, 213–233.

Warr, P., M. Bird and N. Rackham (1970) *Evaluation of Management Training*, Gower Press, London.

Weinstein, L.M. and E.S. Kasl (1982) 'How the training dollar is spent', *Training and Development Journal*, October.

Wetzel, S., P. Konoske and W. Montague (1983) *Estimating Skills Loss through a Navy Technical Pipeline*, NPRDC TR 84–7 (Navy Personnel Research and Development Center, San Diego, California).

Woodman R.W. and J.J. Sherwood (1980) 'The role of team development in organizational effectiveness: a critical review', *Psychological Bulletin*, **88**, 1, 166–186.

Woodward N. (1975) Cost-Benefit Analysis of Supervisor Training, *Industrial Relations Journal* **6**, 2, 41–47.

Index

Further titles in the McGraw-Hill Training Series